Methods for Improving World Transportation Accounts, Applied to 1950-1953

HERMAN F. KARREMAN

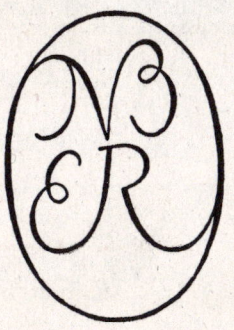

TECHNICAL PAPER/15

NATIONAL BUREAU OF ECONOMIC RESEARCH

Methods for Improving World Transportation Accounts, Applied to 1950-1953

HERMAN F. KARREMAN
Princeton University

TECHNICAL PAPER 15

NATIONAL BUREAU OF ECONOMIC RESEARCH
1961

H11
N2384
no. 15
B/E

Copyright © 1961 by
NATIONAL BUREAU OF ECONOMIC RESEARCH, INC.,
261 Madison Avenue, New York 16, N. Y.

All Rights Reserved

LIBRARY OF CONGRESS CATALOG CARD NUMBER: 60–53380

PRICE: $1.50

Printed in the United States of America
by Quinn & Boden Company, Inc., Rahway, New Jersey

This report is part of a larger investigation of the structure of world trade and payments conducted with the aid of a grant to the National Bureau from the Ford Foundation. The Foundation, of course, is not to be held responsible for any of the statements made or views expressed.

NATIONAL BUREAU OF ECONOMIC RESEARCH
1960

OFFICERS

George B. Roberts, *Chairman*
Arthur F. Burns, *President*
Theodore W. Schultz, *Vice-President*
Murray Shields, *Treasurer*
Solomon Fabricant, *Director of Research*
Geoffrey H. Moore, *Associate Director of Research*
Hal B. Lary, *Associate Director of Research*
William J. Carson, *Executive Director*

DIRECTORS AT LARGE

Wallace J. Campbell, *Nationwide Insurance*
Solomon Fabricant, *New York University*
Crawford H. Greenewalt, *E. I. du Pont de Nemours & Company*
Gabriel Hauge, *Manufacturers Trust Company*
Albert J. Hettinger, Jr., *Lazard Frères and Company*
H. W. Laidler, *League for Industrial Democracy*
Shepard Morgan, *Norfolk, Connecticut*
George B. Roberts, *Larchmont, New York*
Harry Scherman, *Book-of-the-Month Club*
Boris Shishkin, *American Federation of Labor and Congress of Industrial Organizations*
George Soule, *South Kent, Connecticut*
J. Raymond Walsh, *New York City*
Joseph H. Willits, *Armonk, New York*
Leo Wolman, *Columbia University*
Donald B. Woodward, *Richardson-Merrell Inc.*
Theodore O. Yntema, *Ford Motor Company*

DIRECTORS BY UNIVERSITY APPOINTMENT

V. W. Bladen, *Toronto*
Arthur F. Burns, *Columbia*
Lester V. Chandler, *Princeton*
Melvin G. de Chazeau, *Cornell*
Frank W. Fetter, *Northwestern*
Harold M. Groves, *Wisconsin*

Gottfried Haberler, *Harvard*
Walter W. Heller, *Minnesota*
Maurice W. Lee, *North Carolina*
Lloyd G. Reynolds, *Yale*
Theodore W. Schultz, *Chicago*
Willis J. Winn, *Pennsylvania*

DIRECTORS BY APPOINTMENT OF OTHER ORGANIZATIONS

Percival F. Brundage, *American Institute of Certified Public Accountants*
Harold G. Halcrow, *American Farm Economic Association*
Theodore V. Houser, *Committee for Economic Development*
S. H. Ruttenberg, *American Federation of Labor and Congress of Industrial Organizations*
Murray Shields, *American Management Association*
Willard L. Thorp, *American Economic Association*
W. Allen Wallis, *American Statistical Association*
Harold F. Williamson, *Economic History Association*

DIRECTORS EMERITI

Oswald W. Knauth, *Beaufort, South Carolina*   N. I. Stone, *New York City*

RESEARCH STAFF

Moses Abramovitz
Gary S. Becker
William H. Brown, Jr.
Gerhard Bry
Arthur F. Burns
Phillip Cagan
Joseph W. Conard
Morris A. Copeland
Frank G. Dickinson
James S. Earley
Richard A. Easterlin
Solomon Fabricant

Milton Friedman
Raymond W. Goldsmith
Millard Hastay
Daniel M. Holland
Thor Hultgren
F. Thomas Juster
C. Harry Kahn
John W. Kendrick
Simon Kuznets
Hal B. Lary
Robert E. Lipsey
Ruth P. Mack
Jacob Mincer

Ilse Mintz
Geoffrey H. Moore
Roger F. Murray
Ralph L. Nelson
G. Warren Nutter
Richard T. Selden
Lawrence H. Seltzer
Robert P. Shay
George J. Stigler
Norman B. Ture
Leo Wolman
Herbert B. Woolley

RELATION OF THE DIRECTORS TO THE WORK AND PUBLICATIONS OF THE NATIONAL BUREAU OF ECONOMIC RESEARCH

1. The object of the National Bureau of Economic Research is to ascertain and to present to the public important economic facts and their interpretation in a scientific and impartial manner. The Board of Directors is charged with the responsibility of ensuring that the work of the National Bureau is carried on in strict conformity with this object.

2. To this end the Board of Directors shall appoint one or more Directors of Research.

3. The Director or Directors of Research shall submit to the members of the Board, or to its Executive Committee, for their formal adoption, all specific proposals concerning researches to be instituted.

4. No report shall be published until the Director or Directors of Research shall have submitted to the Board a summary drawing attention to the character of the data and their utilization in the report, the nature and treatment of the problems involved, the main conclusions, and such other information as in their opinion would serve to determine the suitability of the report for publication in accordance with the principles of the National Bureau.

5. A copy of any manuscript proposed for publication shall also be submitted to each member of the Board. For each manuscript to be so submitted a special committee shall be appointed by the President, or at his designation by the Executive Director, consisting of three Directors selected as nearly as may be one from each general division of the Board. The names of the special manuscript committee shall be stated to each Director when the summary and report described in paragraph (4) are sent to him. It shall be the duty of each member of the committee to read the manuscript. If each member of the special committee signifies his approval within thirty days, the manuscript may be published. If each member of the special committee has not signified his approval within thirty days of the transmittal of the report and manuscript, the Director of Research shall then notify each member of the Board, requesting approval or disapproval of publication, and thirty additional days shall be granted for this purpose. The manuscript shall then not be published unless at least a majority of the entire Board and a two-thirds majority of those members of the Board who shall have voted on the proposal within the time fixed for the receipt of votes on the publication proposed shall have approved.

6. No manuscript may be published, though approved by each member of the special committee, until forty-five days have elapsed from the transmittal of the summary and report. The interval is allowed for the receipt of any memorandum of dissent or reservation, together with a brief statement of his reasons, that any member may wish to express; and such memorandum of dissent or reservation shall be published with the manuscript if he so desires. Publication does not, however, imply that each member of the Board has read the manuscript, or that either members of the Board in general, or of the special committee, have passed upon its validity in every detail.

7. A copy of this resolution shall, unless otherwise determined by the Board, be printed in each copy of every National Bureau book.

(Resolution adopted October 25, 1926 and revised February 6, 1933 and February 24, 1941)

Contents

	PAGE
Acknowledgments	xi
Foreword by Herbert B. Woolley	xiii
Introduction	1
1. The Existing Records	3
The System of Reporting	3
The Reported Figures	10
2. Amplification of the Records	13
Freight on Imports	13
Unreported Ship Earnings and Disbursements	27
Tankers Operated by British Oil Companies	28
Ships under Flags of Convenience	31
The Greek Fleet	40
Miscellaneous	42
Receipts from Sales of Fuel Out of Bunkers	42
Port Receipts	43
3. The Amplified Records	47
4. Tentative Analysis of the Records	56
5. Methods to Correct Freight Payments	64
6. Methods to Correct Freight Receipts	74
Comparison of French Freight Receipts Over Time	75
Comparison of Scandinavian and United States Freight Receipts	76
Appendix Tables	87

Tables

	PAGE
1. System of Reporting Commodities Bought F.O.B. by Finland from United Kingdom and Carried by a Swedish Vessel to Finland	6
2. Commodities Bought C.I.F. by Finland from United Kingdom and Carried by a Swedish Vessel to Finland	7
3. Receipts from All Transportation Items, World Areas, 1951	11
4. Payments for All Transportation Items, World Areas, 1951	12
5. Freight Rates and C.I.F. Unit Values, Actual Freight Factors, and Freight Factor Indexes, 1950-1953	14
6. Estimated Amount of Freight on Imports and Amount as Percentage of C.I.F. Values, 1950-1953	21
7. Comparison of Allocation of Freight on Imports Paid by Denmark with Flag Distribution of Imported Quantities and of Vessels Calling at Danish Ports, 1951	23
8. Comparison of Allocations of Freight on Imports with Flag Distribution of Imports, Australia 1951, Japan 1953	25
9. Freight on Imports Stated but Unallocated by Importing Country, 1950-1953	26
10. Norwegian Tonnages, Receipts and Payments for International Shipping Activities, 1949-1953	33
11. Tonnages, Receipts and Payments of Norwegian Ships, 1949-1953	35
12. Distribution of Fleets under Flags of Convenience, July 1 of 1950-1953	36
13. Average Speed of Tankers, Selected Dates, 1951-1953	36

Tables

		PAGE
14.	Proportionate Share of Tankers Owned by Oil Companies, Selected Dates, 1951-1953	37
15.	Tonnages of Fleets Carrying Flags of Panama, Honduras, and Liberia Operated on Voyage and on Time Charter, 1950-1953	38
16.	Estimated Receipts and Payments of Fleets Carrying Flags of Panama, Honduras, and Liberia, 1950-1953	39
17.	Tonnages of the Greek Fleet Operated on Voyage Charter and on Time Charter, 1950-1953	40
18.	Estimated Receipts and Payments of Greek Fleet, 1950-1953	41
19.	Port Receipts, Tonnages Entered, and Cargo Delivered and Loaded, Italy and Japan, 1950-1953	45
20.	Adjustments in Transportation Figures, 1951	48
21.	Comparison of Total Receipts and Total Payments of United Kingdom with Total Payments and Total Receipts of Partner Areas	50
22.	Comparison Between Payments and Receipts of All Reporting Countries, 1950-1953	51
23.	Comparison of Payments Reported by Partner Areas with Receipts Reported by the Area, 1950-1953	54
24.	Comparison of Annual Gross Freight Earnings with Size of Fleets, as of July 1	58
25.	Tanker Tonnages and Percentage Proportion in Corresponding Fleets of World Areas, 1950-1953	61
26.	Computation of Quantity of Seaborne Dry Cargo Imported by France, 1950-1953	69
27.	Computed Freight on Imports of France, 1950-1953	70
28.	Computed Freight on Imports of United Kingdom, 1950-1953	72
29.	French Fleet Freight Earnings and Port Payments in Foreign Currency, 1950-1953	76
30.	Derivation of Average Foreign Trade Freight Earnings of Dry Cargo Vessels Operated by Residents of Norway, Sweden, and Denmark, 1950-1953	78
31.	Derivation of Average Foreign Trade Freight Earnings of Dry Cargo Ships Operated by United States Residents, 1950-1953	82

Appendix Tables

	PAGE
A-1. Allocation of Freight on Imports Estimated by NBER, 1950-1953	87
A-2. Freight on Imports, Stated by Country but Allocated by NBER, 1950-1953	95
A-3. Receipts and Payments in Foreign Exchange by United Kingdom for Tanker Operations, 1950-1953	98
A-4. Earnings and Running Expenses of Vessels Flying the Flags of Panama, Honduras, and Liberia, 1950-1953	100
A-5. Earnings and Running Expenses of Greek Fleet, 1950-1953	102
A-6. Estimated Receipts for Sale of Fuel from Bunkers Assumed Not Reported, 1950-1953	104
A-7. Estimated Port Receipts, Assumed Not Reported, 1950-1953	108
A-8. Receipts and Payments, Revised, All Items and All Areas, 1950-1953	110
A-9. Receipts and Payments, Revised, Gross Freight, All Areas, 1950-1953	114
A-10. Receipts and Payments, Revised, Nonfreight Items, All Areas, 1950-1953	118

Acknowledgments

I welcome this opportunity to express my appreciation for the support I received in one form or another from Herbert B. Woolley at various stages of the study. In addition, the results of Cornelius J. Dwyer's study of international petroleum transactions were useful in preparing the section on tankers.

I am indebted to Jon O. Norbom and Robert Stern for their assistance in the more laborious parts of the study, to Walther P. Michael for his precise collection of data from the International Monetary Fund files, and to Carmellah Moneta for performing a good deal of the computations.

The critical comments of Douglass C. North, and in particular those of Thor Hultgren, both of whom reviewed an earlier draft of this paper, proved to be most helpful in preparing the final version of this manuscript. I should like to acknowledge the comments made by the members of the reading committee of the National Bureau's Board of Directors: Melvin G. de Chazeau, Shepard Morgan, and Lloyd G. Reynolds. I am indebted also to Margaret T. Edgar, whose editing improved the readability of this paper.

The first results of this study were given in a paper submitted for discussion to a conference on international economics, called by the Universities-National Bureau Committee for Economic Research, April 1956. An abstract of it appeared with the other papers and abstracts of the conference in the *Review of Economics and Statistics,* February 1958 Supplement.

Foreword

International trade involves more than the exchange of goods valued f.o.b. the frontier of the selling country; in the usual case some expense must be incurred by either the buyer or seller in transporting the goods over water and occasionally overland through third countries. Sometimes the importing country calls for the goods; sometimes the seller delivers, and sometimes vessels operated by residents of third countries or the rail facilities of an inland country like Switzerland will be employed in moving goods between countries. International trade without charges for movement between frontiers is largely confined to trade between contiguous continental countries in Europe and North America. Even a good part of the United States–Canadian trade involves carriage over the Great Lakes, and some trade between contiguous countries on the Continent moves down the Rhine, coastwise, or along inland waterways.

Where the purchasing country provides the transportation between frontiers no international transaction arises. The productive activity is regarded as domestic. However, where the buying country employs the services of residents either in the supplying country or in third countries the purchase of services is as much a part of the international division of labor as the purchase of the goods is. Indeed, some countries specialize in supplying transportation services to other countries: over half of all goods and services credits realized by Greece and nearly half earned by Norway over the five years 1950-1954 were on transportation account. Panama owes its very existence as an independent state to the favorable geographic setting which it affords for transportation, and the hopes of Egypt for betterment have been placed in part upon turning its similar geographic position to better advantage.

Not only may international transactions be required for the carriage of goods traded, but shipping companies serving the world's transit routes also incur a variety of operating expenditures in connection with their business, only some of which may be made at home. Port charges for stevedoring, payments for ships' stores, bunkers, wages of seamen, repairs, and canal fees are important international transactions. Since these are

Foreword

intimately associated with the movement of goods between countries they, as well as charges for freight, are considered "transportation" transactions. The whole set of such transactions has a particular meaning: it makes up the internationally exchanged receipts and current expenditures of a single, well-defined, industry—the shipping industry. The services rendered by and to this industry in world commerce represent the largest of the services normally distinguished in international payments accounts, and a larger total of expenditures and receipts than that for any product distinguished in the Standard International Trade Classification three-digit groupings. Indeed, at approximately 10 per cent of world trade over the five years 1950-1954, transportation transactions represented a contribution to world trade about as large as the f.o.b. value of all petroleum moving between countries.

Because of its magnitude and identification with a particular economic activity, an account of the transportation transactions between world areas affords a promising unit for special study. Given such an account, one would have the essential record for describing and analyzing the character of specialization in supplying the most important of all internationally traded services, for the working out of rivalry in competition between supplying areas, for exploring the financial consequences of government policies favoring national shipping industries, and for spelling out the financial impact of disruptions to world trade like that caused by the closure of the Suez Canal in 1956-1957. But where is such a record to be found?

Before we at the National Bureau undertook to compile a record of transactions of different types between world areas, no one had published an account of the transactions between world areas on account of transportation—and for good reason! Such an account cannot be put together by a simple compilation of entries in the published payments accounts of all countries of the world. A compilation, involving the conversion of values from currency units employed in country accounts to a common *numeraire*, is a sizable task for any one year. But intricate accounting problems, related to the ways in which countries account for their merchandise transactions and offshore activities, must be resolved. Such important sections of the world's transportation account as British tanker transactions, transactions of the fleets of Panama, Honduras, and Liberia (PHL), and the Greek fleet are not reported in official accounts; bunkers and port receipts are not always reported; and transactions are not always allocated by partner area. Moreover, most countries of the world maintain trade records with merchandise imports valued c.i.f. and do not distinguish payments for freight.

A reporting country that is small and underdeveloped and lacks the

Foreword

means of carrying its own goods may find it convenient to draw up its payments accounts with the cost of insurance and freight included as part of merchandise value. No domestic transactions will be included in its record of payments if it carries none of the imported goods, and only a small overstatement of international transactions will usually be involved if it carries some. To maintain balance in its accounts in the latter case, the practice of such countries is to count payments to domestic carriers also as receipts in the shipping account. While payments accounts thus compiled serve a useful purpose in analyzing the international financial position of individual countries, they violate the cardinal principle to be respected in constructing two-valued matrixes of transactions of any given type between world areas, namely: *all transactions of the given type should be shown in the same category by all countries and both the debiting and crediting countries should enter a given transaction in the same category.*

With Walther P. Michael's assistance, in 1954 I undertook a preliminary reconnaissance of the transportation transactions carried in official payments accounts. The resulting "Trial Run Matrix of Transportation Transactions between World Areas in 1951" (NBER, 1954, mimeograph) led to the conclusion that more careful study should be given to transportation. As Americans were poorly versed in European shipping practices, we looked abroad for *expertise* and found it at the Netherlands Central Planning Bureau. Herman F. Karreman was invited to undertake a special study of the world's transportation transactions as part of the more comprehensive study of the structure of world trade and payments being carried on at the National Bureau with aid from the Ford Foundation. This technical paper is the result of that special study.

In setting out on a study of the structure of world trade and payments we have sought to realize statistical, descriptive, and analytical objectives. The statistical objectives were to explore the problems of preparing, with the resources available, the best possible record of international transactions of different types between world areas, to assess the limitations of the data for different purposes, and to prescribe ways to improve the record. The descriptive objectives were to examine the record thus prepared and to observe the economic relationships. The analytical objectives were to employ the record to develop a greater insight into the behavior of the world economy in the past and its likely performance in the future.

Our study of transportation transactions has contributed mainly to realizing objectives of the first two kinds. We have, from Karreman's work reported on in this paper, a full delineation of the problems of setting down a record of transportation transactions between world areas, a contribution of new estimates which notably improve the record, and

Foreword

an indication of ways in which the major remaining deficiencies in the estimation of gross freights might be reduced.

In my further study of transportation transactions employing Karreman's results and also later estimates for the period 1950-1954 (an analysis to be incorporated in the report on the whole study), we have an indication of the limitations of the data for descriptive purposes. Despite the remaining deficiencies in accounting, I find the record usable for some descriptive purposes.

One can gain from the record a considerable insight into the main features of trading in transportation services by world areas and between areas. The broad structure of gross trade in transport services is revealed by the accounts—the concentration of supply, the orientation of particular areas toward certain centers, the comparatively weak position of the United States as a supplier, and the comparative unimportance of most trades between peripheral areas.

We can observe, although imperfectly because of the shortness of the time series, the broad trend of developments over a period of years in the trade in transportation services, reflecting as they do the growth of fleets under different flags. Continental OEEC and PHL fleets show a marked growth, which can be observed in the four years covered by Karreman's study and which continued on into 1954. The growth is reflected in the gain in net transportation trading by the Continent over the years 1950-1954 with all areas and with most partner areas, but particularly with the U.S. The Continent's gain tended to be at the expense of the U.S.

A marked cyclical swing in trade in transportation is apparent in the series I have studied for the five years 1950-1954. The swing for all transportation transactions was more marked than the similar swing in goods trade, and one can observe, particularly for the larger interarea trades, how the general swing in transportation transactions affected particular interarea relationships. The U.S. gained initially from nearly all areas in 1951, the European centers tended to gain from peripheral areas, and the Continent gained from the U.K. The direction of year-to-year change in interarea gross and net trades of transportation are imperfectly recorded by both sides but, with the bias in reporting systematic, the general character of the changes can be observed.

These broad features can be measured to within fairly narrow limits, but not so narrow as for merchandise. The data show a general tendency for transportation payments to be consistently reported in excess of credits acknowledged, a feature seemingly related cyclically to the swing in world confidence associated with the Korean war. There is the suggestion in the figures that the transportation account, particularly of the Continental OEEC countries, provided a major source of leakage in foreign exchange during the early 1950's. An audit of freight payments along

Foreword

the lines Karreman proposes would help establish whether the fault lies with the process of statistical estimation or with the records of exchange controls on the Continent.

It is my observation that errors in the accounts, while sizable, do not render them unusable for describing and measuring the order of magnitude of movements, from year to year and over the five years, in net transportation balances and net transportation balances between areas where the balance is large. Paired records of year-to-year change and change over the five years do not agree so well on the magnitude of change in balance as on the direction of change. But paired records do usually agree on the direction and roughly on the magnitude of the annual balance between areas. The pattern of net balances between world areas has persisted from year to year with little change. The most marked development over the five years has been the growth of the Continental fleet and the improvement of its trading position particularly with the U.S.

These features of the trade in transportation in the years 1950-1954 are not vitiated by the record which must be recognized as being subject to considerable over-all error even after the extensive adjustments made by Karreman. At the same time the two-valued matrix provides a basis for observing at which points the record appears to be particularly deficient. Those using the record in analysis have some indication of the extent of its deficiencies and some indication from Karreman's work as to how some remaining deficiencies might be corrected (see especially Sections 5 and 6).

Whether it is worthwhile for others to undertake the further task of improving the record would depend, of course, upon the analytic uses to which it was to be put. As noted above, our interest has been to develop a serviceable set of accounts for different types of transactions with a view to observing the nature and changing character of specialization in trade between world areas. We have sought with limited resources to develop the best possible record to serve that purpose, and for that purpose, as we have noted, the imperfect record can be used. It can also be useful to obtain indications of the financial consequences of such a disruption to world trade as occurred with the closing of the Suez Canal in 1956-1957. From the pattern of net trade in transportation it seems clear that the burden of higher cost transportation was borne by the peripheral areas that were compelled to pay higher freight costs while, ironically, the North Atlantic centers supplying shipping tended to gain. This much can be inferred from the 1950-1954 record and even more could undoubtedly be said from similar accounts for later years if they were available. A precise measure of the costs and gains from the Suez crisis might be dependent upon a further improvement in the accounts.

HERBERT B. WOOLLEY

June 1960

Introduction

The International Monetary Fund (IMF) collects, year by year, information on the international transactions of its member countries. The part of this information that refers to transportation activities is the subject of this study.

In Section 1, an exposition is given of the material as secured from the IMF files, which automatically leads to a discussion of the main deficiencies in the reporting.

The second section describes the ways used in this study to fill some of the biggest gaps in the information without, however, making any changes in the reported figures.

The amplified records, presented in Section 3, show big surpluses of payments over receipts. The gross freight, having been separated out, was found to account for most of the discrepancies, rather than the other transportation items.

A tentative analysis of the records in their present form is given in Section 4. No far-reaching conclusions could be drawn because of the remaining discrepancies between payments and receipts as well as the lack of information on chartering.

Methods to correct the figures on payments and receipts are presented in Sections 5 and 6. No use was made of the checks provided by the system of reporting, as such, because so far the number of countries that comply with the requirements is too small.

1

The Existing Records

THE SYSTEM OF REPORTING

To appraise the information on transportation activities requires knowledge of the system of reporting. IMF's *Balance of Payments Manual* supplies the member countries with a consistent set of rules for reporting their international transactions. The manual, published in January 1950, sets forth the underlying principles, the system of reporting, and general instructions for its use. Tables with detailed information are given for the main components of the balance of payments, of which transportation is one. It is not the intention to deal extensively here with the system of reporting, but only to draw attention to certain aspects of it that bear upon the quality of the transportation figures. These are variations in the way of reporting: the value of imports and exports; the revenues and payments for transport of commodities between other countries—"cross trade"; and the receipts and payments for other activities associated with transportation.

While the IMF uses in the balance of payments f.o.b. values for both imports and exports, countries vary in their choice of values reported. The result is a lack of uniformity in the transportation account. There is a close relationship between the reporting of transportation transactions and that of merchandise transactions. The latter is based on the invoices accompanying the commodities on their way from seller to buyer and stating the amounts of the transactions subject to varying specified conditions. In many cases the invoice shows the f.o.b. (free on board) value of the commodities, or the value at the time the commodities leave the country of export. In others, the invoice shows the c.i.f. (cost, insurance, and freight) value of the commodities, or the value up to the time the commodities are delivered in a port of the importing

The Existing Records

country. The question therefore arises which of the two commodity values is most suitable to be shown in a uniform system of reporting.

From the point of view of customs collection, the most interesting statistics are the f.o.b. value of exports and the c.i.f. value of imports. These values are the basis of duties and consequently must be reported in customs returns. The customs returns are the basis of the foreign trade statistics, which also usually state the f.o.b. value of exports and the c.i.f. value of imports. Some countries, however, manage to deduct the freight charges from the c.i.f. value of the imported merchandise, leaving its f.o.b. value. In those instances, it is possible to record the same value, i.e. the f.o.b. value, of the merchandise by both exporting and importing countries.

This possibility is probably the main reason for the Fund's decision in favor of showing the f.o.b. value of exports as well as imports in the balance of payments. Comparison of the two sets of values reveals inconsistencies in the reporting. In addition, if not only the total amounts of exports and imports are shown but also their allocation to partner areas, a useful tool will be forged for bringing the receipts and payments figures to agreement and achieving a true balance of payments.

Another reason for deciding in favor of the f.o.b. value of imports could have been that useful information on transportation transactions, apart from that on merchandise transactions, could be secured. Hence, the IMF's choice was a happy one, capable of providing us with the maximum information attainable. This means, however, that countries whose customs returns show the c.i.f. value of their imports have to estimate each year the freight (and other additional costs) incorporated in that value—a costly and time-consuming task if done accurately. This poses the question whether putting the customs returns for imports also directly on an f.o.b. basis would not pay. It would eliminate inconsistencies in the reporting which are otherwise difficult to remove, as shown by a simple example.

Let us assume, for instance, that Finland buys commodities in the United Kingdom for 90 currency units and that the merchandise is carried by a Swedish vessel to Finland for an additional 10 currency units.[1] Two tables show for each of the three countries:

1. The actual transactions (as might be reflected by exchange control records)
2. The adjustments to be made by each country to fit its system of reporting

[1] All three countries state the f.o.b. value for the exports and the c.i.f. value for the imports in their trade statistics.

The Existing Records

3. The initial position on the merchandise or transportation line or both of each country's balance of payments
4. The adjustments necessary to bring the balance of payments in correspondence with IMF instructions
5. The ultimate position on both lines of each country's balance of payments

To show the difference made in the recording at the start and the adjustment required thereafter for commodities bought f.o.b. and c.i.f., Table 1 gives the method of reporting for commodities bought f.o.b., and Table 2 for commodities bought c.i.f.

The case in Table 1 is the least complicated of the two, even though the c.i.f. value of the imported merchandise is recorded in Finland's import statistics. The position at the end is the same as at the start, as it should be, since the actual transactions fit exactly the intention of the rules given in the IMF *Manual*.[2]

To take into account that exports are valued f.o.b. in the United Kingdom's trade statistics, Table 2 shows the various stages in the recording until the ultimate balance of payments position has been arrived at. It is somewhat surprising that in this case the positions in the third phase and at the end are not the same as those shown in Table 1. The difference is not important for the United Kingdom, since the debit and credit entries for transportation could eventually cancel each other. Such a cancellation is recommended by the IMF *Manual*, . . . "on the assumption that the exporter acts merely as an agent for the foreign importer."[3] The final positions of Finland and Sweden on the transportation line in Table 2 differ, however, from those shown in Table 1. For the c.i.f. commodities, Finland's transportation debit is allocated to the United Kingdom, although the commodities were not carried by a British vessel. Also, Sweden's transportation credit is allocated to the United Kingdom, although Finland paid the freight ultimately. An extra entry in the transportation accounts of both countries is needed here to arrive at the same results as in Table 1.

But both countries need more information to make the appropriate correction. The importing country (Finland in our example) needs exact information for deducting the freight charges from the c.i.f. value of its imports and for allocating them to the country that rendered the transportation service. Obviously, the shortest route to that end is for the importing country to report the f.o.b. value of its imports in its balance

[2] *Balance of Payments Manual* (International Monetary Fund), 1950 (hereafter cited as IMF *Manual*).
[3] IMF *Manual*, Section 4, subsection c, p. 3.

The Existing Records

TABLE 1

System of Reporting Commodities Bought F.O.B. by Finland from United Kingdom and Carried by a Swedish Vessel to Finland

| | FINLAND ||||||| UNITED KINGDOM ||||||| SWEDEN ||||||
| | Total || United Kingdom || Sweden || Total || Finland || Sweden || Total || Finland || United Kingdom ||
	C	D	C	D	C	D	C	D	C	D	C	D	C	D	C	D	C	D
1. Actual transactions																		
Merchandise		90		90			90		90									
Transportation		10				10								10		10		
2. Adjustment made by importing country																		
Merchandise	+10		+10															
Transportation	−10		−10															
3. Initial balance of payments position																		
Merchandise	100		100					90		90								
Transportation		10		10		10								10		10		
4. Adjustments to be made for IMF																		
Merchandise	−10		−10															
Transportation	+10		+10															
5. Ultimate balance of payments position																		
Merchandise	90		90					90		90								
Transportation		10				10								10		10		

In this and Table 2, C = credit, D = debit.

TABLE 2
Commodities Bought C.I.F. by Finland from United Kingdom and Carried by a Swedish Vessel to Finland

	FINLAND							UNITED KINGDOM							SWEDEN			
	Total		United Kingdom		Sweden		Total		Finland		Sweden		Total		Finland		United Kingdom	
	C	D	C	D	C	D	C	D	C	D	C	D	C	D	C	D	C	D
1. Actual transactions																		
Merchandise	100		100				100		100									
Transportation								10				10		10				10
2. Adjustments made by exporting country																		
Merchandise	−10		−10				−10		−10									
Transportation	+10		+10				+10		+10									
3. Initial balance of payments position																		
Merchandise	100		100				90		90									
Transportation		10						10		10		10		10				10
4. Adjustments to be made for IMF																		
Merchandise	−10		−10															
Transportation	+10		+10															
5. Ultimate balance of payments position																		
Merchandise	90		90				90		90									
Transportation		10		10				10		10		10		10				10

The Existing Records

of payments. In general, however, the added information required to make the appropriate corrections will not be available. Consequently, the transportation figures in the ultimate balance of payments position of the importing country (Finland) will not be in line with those of the transporting country (Sweden), and an inconsistency remains in the reporting.[4]

The transportation figures in the ultimate balance of payments positions, derived from different sources and by different means, therefore, differ greatly in quality. It is by and large poor in cases where commodities are bought c.i.f.: the final figures are then usually only estimates. For example, unless the Finnish customs keeps accurate records of the freight incorporated in the c.i.f. value of imported merchandise, the debit figure on the transportation line of the ultimate balance of payments can only be estimated by using information on "similar" f.o.b. imports. The transportation figure in the Swedish balance of payments has, on the other hand, a much more exact figure stemming from exchange control records of the amount actually received. The estimated figure in the Finnish balance of payments can only by chance be the same as the actual figure in the Swedish balance of payments. In evaluating the accuracy of all c.i.f.-f.o.b. adjustments of import values made by the countries themselves, this lack of consistency must be borne in mind.

Apart from freight on exports and imports, a country's merchant fleet obtains revenues from transportation of commodities between other countries, too. The income from "cross trade" is for certain countries a multiple of the freight earnings on exports and imports together, and must therefore be included in this discussion of transportation receipts and payments between countries. What is the source of information on receipts from cross trade and what is the quality of the figures? Ordinarily, the figures are supplied by the central banks (particularly in countries with exchange control systems) which obtain them from the shipping companies. An over-all check on the figures, like that on the earnings from exports and imports with the aid of customs returns, is impossible, because the amounts paid by other countries to the shipping companies of the transporting country are so far not available. Consequently, the central banks must either rely on the accuracy of their countries' shipping companies or—in countries with exchange control systems—make costly special investigations of suspected statements. In practice, the figures relating to earnings from cross trade are usually taken at face value and put into the country's balance of payments.

[4] The inconsistency in reporting commodities bought c.i.f. will not be present if the imported merchandise is carried by the importing country's own vessels.

8

The Existing Records

In addition to payments and receipts for freight, there are also those from other transportation activities that affect the balance of payments. On the earnings side are carrying foreign passengers, chartering ships to foreign countries, and some other activities that yield receipts which should be reported on the transportation line of the balance of payments. There are also various kinds of disbursements—port and harbor dues, costs of loading and unloading in foreign ports, wages of nonresidents, and so on.[5] Such payments must be reported not only as transportation debits in the balance of payments of the carriers' countries, but also as credits by the countries receiving them.

Bunker fuel loaded in ports of one country by carriers of other countries must also be reported. The intakes nearly always appear under the transportation debits in the balance of payments of the carriers' countries. Deliveries of bunker fuel can also be regarded as exports of a commodity and are sometimes reported as merchandise. The IMF requires, however, that deliveries of bunker fuel should also be reported under transportation, which helps to balance the transportation debits and credits of all countries together.

The way in which two other items—passenger fares and insurance of commodities—lying on the periphery of transportation are dealt with can also cause some inconsistency in the reporting of transportation transactions in the balance of payments. Passenger fares paid to foreign shipping and aviation companies should be recorded under transportation, as passenger fare receipts are, according to the IMF instructions. To meet these requirements, the countries have to single out passenger fares for overseas ship and air traffic from the other expenditures of their residents abroad. The latter, including passenger fares inside foreign countries, must be reported under travel. Not all countries succeed in making the separation, and part of the overseas ship and plane passenger fares are reported under travel instead of transportation.

The ways of dealing with amounts paid and received for insurance of commodities moved in international trade are another cause of inconsistency in the reporting of transportation transactions. Views differ whether payment of such insurance premiums should be reported under transportation or insurance. The most common opinion seems to be that, since they are closely related to the transportation of commodities, the former is the suitable category. But, in order to keep the world transportation account in balance, at least theoretically, it then becomes necessary to separate receipts for such insurance from receipts for capital goods and life insurance. Commodity insurance should then be reported

---

[5] For detailed description of the various components of the IMF transportation account, see IMF *Manual*.

The Existing Records

under transportation and the other two under insurance—a difficult division to make for proper entries in the balance of payments.

With this brief review of the implications of the system of reporting on the transportation figures, let us now see to what extent countries fulfill the requirements.

THE REPORTED FIGURES

The information on transportation gathered from the IMF's *Balance of Payments Yearbook* [6] (Volumes V and VI), supplemented with some information on details from its files, reveals that up to the present not many countries have succeeded in carrying out the IMF's instructions. Only a few show allocation to partner countries of total amounts as well as of gross freights—by far the most important of all transportation items. Among the thirteen to sixteen member countries that in 1950-1953, had fleets of 1,000 gross register tons (GRT) and over, only the United States, Canada, Denmark, and Japan supplied all the required information on transportation transactions. Other major transportation countries show amounts of freight not allocated to partner countries and totals for all items together; others show only total amounts with allocation; and some only allocation of net amounts (total debits minus credits). Some of the less important countries do considerably better.

A number of countries do not even show the correct totals of payments and receipts for a number of reasons: [7]

1. Many countries, not able to establish the f.o.b. value of their imported merchandise, report the c.i.f. value, with no amount on the transportation line for freight on imports.

2. The United Kingdom does not report receipts and payments of its tanker fleet under transportation but includes them with all petroleum transactions reported under miscellaneous.

3. Panama and Honduras do not consider ships of other countries registered under their flags as part of their national economy and hence leave earnings and disbursements of those fleets out of their balance of payments. Liberia submits no balance of payments and, therefore, no financial report on ships carrying its flag.

4. Greece reports only receipts of contributions to seamen's funds,

---

[6] Hereafter referred to as IMF *Yearbook* of the appropriate volume.

[7] A more detailed discussion of the many deficiencies in the world's transportation accounts can be found in "A Trial-Run Matrix of Transportation Transactions between World Areas in 1951," MS. by Herbert Woolley and Walther P. Michael, National Bureau of Economic Research, 1954.

The Existing Records

seamen's remittances, taxes, profits, and so forth—only the smaller part of the net earnings of the Greek fleet which operates mainly from foreign bases; a very large share of earnings and expenses is not reported by Greece.

5. Since expenses for bunker fuel are part of a ship's disbursements and always reported under transportation debits, receipts for the sale of bunker fuel should logically be reported under transportation credits. Such receipts are not reported by a number of countries, however.

6. The overseas territories of the United Kingdom, France, the Netherlands, Portugal, and Spain do not report receipts for harbor and port dues, fees for loading and unloading, stevedorage, and so forth.

These omissions result in understatement of payments on account of 1, of 2 (expenses of the U.K. tanker fleet), of 3 (expenses of fleets carrying the flags of Panama, Honduras, Liberia), and of 4 (disbursements of the Greek fleet). The omissions result also in understatement of receipts on account of the earnings of those fleets (2, 3, and 4) as well as of other earnings (5 and 6). One might expect these omissions to cancel out to a great extent, leaving no large difference between the debits and credits of all countries together. The differences, when all the reported amounts for 1951 are added together, are shown in Tables 3 and 4. The grand totals are close (5,437 and 5,749), and the allocated totals still closer (4,746 and 4,868). The correspondence is less for individual areas, as expected.

TABLE 3

RECEIPTS FROM ALL TRANSPORTATION ITEMS, WORLD AREAS, 1951
(millions of U.S. dollars)

Receipts of:	£ Area	Non-£ EPU [a]	U.S. and Canada	L.A.	Rest of World	Total Allocated	Unallocated	Total
£ area	681	285	243 [b]	55	170	1,434	48	1,482
Non-£ EPU [a]	461	465	245	85	111	1,367	469	1,836
U.S. and Canada	396	618	152	377	173	1,716		1,716
Latin America	2	3	29	12	1	47	84	131
Rest of world	66	64	26	7	19	182	90	272
Total	1,606	1,435	695	536	474	4,746	691	5,437

SOURCE: IMF, *Yearbook* and files.
[a] European Payments Union.
[b] Includes Latin-American dollar countries and Liberia.

The Existing Records

TABLE 4

PAYMENTS FOR ALL TRANSPORTATION ITEMS, WORLD AREAS, 1951
(millions of U.S. dollars)

	\multicolumn{5}{c}{Payments of:}	
Payments to:	£ Area	Non-£ EPU [a]	U.S. and Canada	L.A.	Rest of World	Total
£ area	581	429	232	31	63	1,336
Non-£ EPU [a]	425	596	335	80	99	1,535
U.S. and Canada	256 [b]	417	185	208	117	1,183
Latin America	36	80	257	17	34	424
Rest of world	92	96	136	35	31	390
Total allocated	1,390	1,618	1,145	371	344	4,868
Unallocated	121	496		210	54	881
Total	1,511	2,114	1,145	581	398	5,749

SOURCE: IMF, *Yearbook* and files.
[a] European Payments Union.
[b] Includes Latin American dollar countries and Liberia.

There is a considerable understatement of receipts and of payments, for reasons noted. On the payments side, for instance, adjustment of imports from c.i.f. to f.o.b. value, alone, amounts to about $2 billion, in addition to omitted expenses of certain fleets. The total effect of the omissions on each side of the combined balance of payments lies between $2.5 and $3 billion in 1951, as will be shown later. For the years under study, no more than about two-thirds of receipts and payments were reported. The next section describes the measures used to amplify the records.

2

Amplification of the Records

To eliminate the gaps in the reporting, estimates were computed for the freight on imports for a number of countries, the earnings and disbursements of some fleets, and the port receipts of some other countries. In addition, the totals have been allocated to areas. No efforts were made to correct the figures submitted by the countries themselves.[8] Consequently the end product is a set of figures that is more or less complete but far from faultless.

FREIGHT ON IMPORTS

More than half the reporting countries state the c.i.f. value of imported merchandise in their balances of payments and, unlike countries reporting imports f.o.b., show no freight on the debit side of the transportation line. To arrive at a set of uniform—f.o.b.—figures for all countries, the freight on imports had to be estimated for the c.i.f. reporting countries. The total amount of freight was subtracted from the c.i.f. value of imported merchandise and added to the transportation debits. Finally, the freight payments were allocated to the countries that rendered the transportation services.

The best method of estimating the freight on imports of a particular country—closest to that actually used by countries reporting it—would be to make a selection of the imported quantities and multiply each by its appropriate freight rate. Because of time-consuming details, it was not possible to apply this method to all countries that do not state the freight on their imports. Section 5 deals more extensively with this accurate method of assessing the freight on imports. In this study a quicker but rougher method was used. The first step is to make a selection of the

[8] The IMF is still not in a position to audit figures submitted by its member countries.

TABLE 5
FREIGHT RATES AND C.I.F. UNIT VALUES, ACTUAL FREIGHT FACTORS, AND FREIGHT FACTOR INDEXES, 1950-1953
(U.S. dollars per ton; index, 1951 = 100)

	Crude Petroleum		Fuel Oil	Gasoline	Coal		Iron Ore	
	Venezuela U.K.	Bahrein U.K.	Indonesia Netherlands	Netherlands Antilles Netherlands	Hampton Roads Netherlands	Bristol Channel River Plate	Algeria U.K.	Sierra Leone U.K.
1950								
Freight rate	5.25	7.60	10.20	5.30		6.45	3.30	4.40
C.I.F. value	22.40	20.85	13.20	46.50	3.75		8.50	7.20
Freight factor	0.234	0.365	0.773	0.114			0.389	0.612
Index	69	71	86	61			72	77
1951								
Freight rate	9.55	13.10	17.90	9.70	10.70	15.25	7.70	10.00
C.I.F. value	28.20	25.40	20.00	51.75	19.10	36.60	14.15	12.55
Freight factor	0.339	0.516	0.895	0.187	0.560	0.417	0.544	0.796
Index	100	100	100	100	100	100	100	100
1952								
Freight rate	11.90	16.15	22.10	12.10	9.10	12.45	5.00	5.20
C.I.F. value	27.50	27.50	23.40	54.60	18.85	29.20	17.55	14.85
Freight factor	0.432	0.588	0.945	0.221	0.485	0.425	0.285	0.350
Index	127	114	106	118	87	102	53	44
1953								
Freight rate	6.45	9.15	12.40	6.55	4.75	4.90	3.50	4.60
C.I.F. value	25.00	21.95	17.35	56.10	14.60	21.80	16.65	16.05
Freight factor	0.258	0.417	0.715	0.117	0.325	0.225	0.210	0.286
Index	76	81	80	63	58	54	39	41

(continued)

Amplification of the Records

TABLE 5 (concluded)

	Fertilizer Tunisia U.K.	Wheat St. Lawrence U.K.	Wheat Australia U.K.	Maize River Plate Netherlands	Timber Finland Netherlands	Lumber Canada (Pacific) Netherlands	Sugar Cuba U.K.
1950							
Freight rate	3.60	5.40	9.90	6.90	4.35	10.25	8.20
C.I.F. value	12.30	81.00	73.50	65.50	29.40	113.50	122.00
Freight factor	0.293	0.067	0.135	0.105	0.148	0.090	0.067
Index	70	39	58	76	72	54	48
1951							
Freight rate	8.30	15.00	19.90	14.45	8.50	24.00	19.55
C.I.F. value	19.75	87.00	85.50	104.00	41.40	142.50	139.00
Freight factor	0.420	0.173	0.233	0.139	0.205	0.168	0.140
Index	100	100	100	100	100	100	100
1952							
Freight rate	5.25	7.20	13.60	9.00	5.55	15.90	12.25
C.I.F. value	20.90	86.80	85.80	91.50	46.50	161.50	128.50
Freight factor	0.251	0.083	0.159	0.098	0.119	0.098	0.095
Index	60	48	68	71	58	58	68
1953							
Freight rate	4.65	6.55	11.75	9.55	4.90	10.70	9.30
C.I.F. value	16.90	84.50	83.80	77.80	39.50	149.50	86.00
Freight factor	0.275	0.078	0.140	0.123	0.124	0.072	0.108
Index	65	45	60	88	60	43	77

SOURCE: For freight rates on petroleum, the London Award; for freight rates on dry cargo, publications of the Central Bureaus of Statistics of the Netherlands and the United Kingdom.

Amplification of the Records

imported values by broad commodity groups and to distribute the value in each group over various areas of origin. The next step is to determine the proportion of freight to (c.i.f.) value per unit of quantity of the commodity groups, and to apply those proportions to the corresponding values.[9] The crux was, of course, to establish the freight factors, i.e., the proportions of the freight in the (c.i.f.) unit values—rough though they must be.

In determining these freight factors, use was made of results of previous investigations for the same purpose by the statistical bureaus of France, West Germany, the Netherlands, and Switzerland for 1951 or the first months of 1952.[10] Though the freight factors found for a particular commodity group were not always the same for all four countries, they all lie within a small range. There was little variance in the factors of various groups of high-value commodities no matter from which part of the world they came; for groups of low-value commodities, however, distance had a definite influence on the factors. On the basis of these observations it was assumed that the freight factors for those four West European countries could be used for other countries for which the c.i.f.-f.o.b. adjustments had to be calculated, provided some allowance was made, where necessary, for the length of haul. Occasionally the validity of this assumption was tested by comparing available freight rates with corresponding unit values; in general, it was found that the adopted and adjusted freight factors could be used for making a first estimate of the freight on imports.

Still other aspects of these rough c.i.f.-f.o.b. adjustments had to be taken into account. First, not all imports are sea borne. Sometimes assumptions had to be made about the means of transportation used, by considering mainly the parts of the two countries where a commodity was produced and had its destination, the existing ways of transportation between them, and so on. In certain instances, where the exporting and importing country are contiguous, no freight has to be deducted from the value of the merchandise. According to the IMF rules, both exported and imported merchandise should be valued at the frontier of the country of export, which between bordering countries is also the frontier of the country of import. Sometimes, however, it must be assumed that the commodity did not cross the common border but came by sea, and for

[9] Carmellah Moneta, who had a great share in calculating these c.i.f.-f.o.b. adjustments gives a good description of the method in "The Estimation of Transportation Costs in International Trade Accounts," *Journal of Political Economy*, February 1959.

[10] Obtained from the Statistical Commission and the Economic Commission for Europe of the United Nations (E/CN.3/Conf. 3/L.2), E/ECE/Stat. 3/L.2, Add. 1, June 15, 1953.

Amplification of the Records

such transportation between contiguous countries allowance for freight has been made in the balance of payments of the importing country.

Second, some attention was paid to changes in the 1951 freight factors for estimating the freight on imports for the other years studied. Without exact information on freight rates for most commodities imported by the countries for which c.i.f.-f.o.b. adjustments had to be made, the 1951 freight factors were changed only in a general way. This was necessary particularly for materials for which unit values, freight rates, and hence freight factors fluctuated greatly in those years. The selections included some of the most important raw materials, for which annual freight rates for transportation over particular routes have been secured; their corresponding c.i.f. unit values were computed from data shown in import statistics (see Table 5).

Some interesting features emerge from the table. The freight rates of tankers and dry cargo vessels show a remarkable conformity of movement, as one might expect from prices established on open markets. With the dry cargo rates in 1951 at 100, the indexes are shown in the next tabulation.

	1950	1951	1952	1953
Coal				
Hampton Roads—Netherlands	35	100	85	44
Bristol Channel—River Plate	42	100	82	32
Wheat				
St. Lawrence—United Kingdom	36	100	48	44
Australia—United Kingdom	50	100	68	60
Maize				
River Plate—Netherlands	48	100	62	66
Sugar				
Cuba—United Kingdom	42	100	63	48
Iron Ore				
Algeria—United Kingdom	43	100	65	45
Sierra Leone—United Kingdom	44	100	52	46
Fertilizers				
Tunisia—United Kingdom	43	100	63	56
Timber				
Finland—Netherlands	51	100	65	68
Lumber				
North Pacific—Netherlands	43	100	66	44

The range and central tendency of these rates (except coal) in 1950, 1952, and 1953 are 36-51 and 45 in 1950, 48-68 and 61 in 1952 and 44-68 and 53 in 1953 (particular circumstances prevailing in Europe caused the high coal freight rates in 1951 and 1952). This suggests that, once we know the tramp freight rate of a particular commodity transported over

Amplification of the Records

a certain route for one year, we can estimate the corresponding rates of that commodity for the other years rather well.

As to freight rates: The freight rate per ton of a particular commodity in one year is somewhat proportional to the length of haul to which it applies. The freight rates for cereals, for example, transported from the St. Lawrence, the River Plate, and West Australia to the U.K.–Continent in 1950 are, respectively, $5.40, $6.90 and $9.90 whereas the (approximate) distances are, respectively, 3,000, 5,100 and 9,450 nautical miles.

Comparison of the freight rates of different commodities, however, shows differences that cannot be explained by distance only. The freight rates for cereals from St. Lawrence to the United Kingdom, for timber from Finland to the Netherlands, and for sugar from Cuba to the U.K. in 1950 are, respectively, $5.40, $4.35, and $8.20 per ton, whereas the distances are, respectively, 3,000, 950, and 4,200 nautical miles. Freight rates are not based so much on the weight of freight as on the space occupied—a better measure for the utilization of services offered by the carriers. The relation between the weight and the space occupied by a commodity is given by the so-called stowage factor, which is the number of cubic feet occupied by a long ton (2,240 pounds). The stowage factor for wheat (in bulk) is 48, for timber (air-dried) 66, and for sugar (in bags) 50.[11] If the three freight rates per ton are divided by the stowage factors we obtain the freight rates per cubic foot, for wheat $0.11, for timber $0.07, and for sugar $0.16, which are now in better correspondence with the distances. This distance factor and other factors that determine the freight rates are discussed more extensively in the fifth section.

The freight factors, however, being the quotient of the freight rates and the unit values per ton, show little conformity, even those for a particular commodity in the same year. The 1950 freight factor for iron ore imported by the United Kingdom from Algeria is 0.389, whereas it is 0.613 for iron ore from Sierra Leone. We observe similar differences for other years. Also, the 1950 freight factor for a relatively high-value commodity, wheat imported by the U.K. from the St. Lawrence, is 0.067, whereas it is 0.135 for wheat from Australia. The wide differences are caused by differences not only in the freight rates but also in the c.i.f. unit values of the commodities. Two conclusions can be drawn: it is hazardous to use for a particular commodity always the same freight factor; in fixing freight factors, due account must be taken of the applicable freight rates.

From the roughly computed 1951 freight factors for the most important raw materials imports, the factors of the other years were obtained in a rather general way. Approximately the same proportional changes were

[11] Derived from Joseph Leeming, *Modern Shipping Stowage*, Department of Commerce, 1942.

Amplification of the Records

made in the 1951 freight factors of other countries as shown by those of the United Kingdom and the Netherlands, given in the tabulation below.

	1950	1952	1953
Petroleum, crude	−30%	+20%	−20%
Petroleum products	−25	+15	−30
Coal	−35 (est.)	−5	−40
Ores, low value	−25	−50	−55
Fertilizers	−30	−40	−35
Cereals	−50	−35	−45
Wood products	−35	−40	−45
Sugar	−50	−30	−20

Similar changes in the 1951 freight factors were made also for other raw materials appearing in the selection of commodities imported by countries for which freight on imports had to be estimated.

The 1951 freight factors for semimanufactured and manufactured commodities, mainly transported by liners, were used unchanged for the other years, on the assumption that movements in the c.i.f. unit values of those broad categories of commodities were about the same as those of the liner freights. To illustrate, the tabulation below shows the export unit value indexes of those commodities, computed by the Statistical Office of the United Nations, and the combined index of liner freights for European and overseas routes, computed by the Marine Section of West Germany's Federal Ministry of Transport.[12]

| | United Nations Export Unit Value Indexes of Manufactured Goods || West Germany Liner Freight Indexes of European and Overseas Routes ||
	1950 = 100	1951 = 100	1953 = 100	1951 = 100
1950	100	84	82	80
1951	119	100	103	100
1952	122	103	112	109
1953	117	98	100	97
1954	115	97	96	93

One might wonder whether the German indexes give a good picture of the fluctuations of liner freight rates all over the world. Most liner conferences raised their rates about 15 per cent in the first part of 1951, sometimes followed by a smaller raise six to nine months later, but this will not amount to an average rise of more than 35 per cent from 1950 to 1952 as shown by the German index. Still more surprising is the sharp decline in the German liner freight index after 1952, since not many liner conferences reduced their rates after 1952. In view of this, the assumption seems warranted that there was in those years some parallel

---

[12] Both published quarterly in the *Monthly Bulletin of Statistics*.

Amplification of the Records

in the fluctuations of export unit values of manufactured goods and liner freight rates, though the amplitude of the former could have been somewhat smaller than that of the latter. That difference in amplitude will be less if the movement of the liner freight rates is compared with that of the import unit values, the latter being composed mainly of export unit values and freight rates. Such considerations led, in this phase of the study, to application for the other years of the 1951 freight factors to the semimanufactured and manufactured products. Hence, there is a difference over time in treatment of those commodities and the raw materials because of the difference in the fluctuations of freight rates and unit values of the two groups of commodities in those years.

The result of the computations is shown in Table 6, giving not only dollar amounts of the freight but also the amounts as percentages of the c.i.f. values of imports. In general it can be said that the high percentages indicate a rather large share of imports consisting of raw materials such as petroleum, coal, ores, fertilizers, timber, and cereals—all commodities with high or relatively high freight factors. The low percentages usually indicate that a large share of the imports consists of semimanufactured and manufactured commodities and in some cases, for instance Mexico, that much has been imported from contiguous countries.

The amounts of freight contained in the c.i.f. value of imports, calculated where necessary, were allocated to the countries that rendered the transportation services. The allocation was based on the distribution of imported quantities of commodities according to flags of their carriers —a basis considered best, but far from ideal. The flag of a vessel usually indicates the country of its owner, whereas its operator that receives the freight is often located in a different country. For example, when a vessel is let on charter to a foreign operator, the freight is received by a resident of one country, and the ship flies the flag of another country. Only if a ship is let on a bare-boat charter—a rare occurrence—might the flag of the charterer's country be substituted. Consequently, the method of allocating freight on imports according to the flag of the carrier is subject to error in cases of chartering to operators of other countries.

Misallocation of freight charges is illustrated by the transportation of petroleum products, which occupies a large part of world fleets. United States and United Kingdom oil companies, main petroleum producers, charter every year a large quantity of carrying capacity for the transport of their products. The U.S. charters these vessels mainly from Panama, Honduras, and Liberia; and the U.K. from continental OEEC[13] countries. If freight on imported petroleum products is distributed by flag of carrier, the amounts allocated to Latin America and continental OEEC

[13] Organisation for European Economic Co-operation.

TABLE 6

ESTIMATED AMOUNT OF FREIGHT ON IMPORTS AND AMOUNT AS PERCENTAGE OF C.I.F. VALUES, 1950-1953
(amounts in millions of U.S. dollars)

	1950		1951		1952		1953	
Ireland	$ 43	7.8%	$ 59	10.3%	$ 46	9.5%	$ 44	8.5%
Iceland	2	6						
New Zealand	67	14.5						
Burma	11	8.1	15	7.9	13	7.5	8	7.1
Ceylon	21	8.7	33	10.3	33	9.3	34	8.3
India	94	8.2	182	10.1	151	10.9	110	9.3
Iraq	11	10	14	10	17	10	19	10
Jordan	5	12	5	12	6	12	6	12
Total other £	254		308		266		221	
British OT's	210	6.9	324	7.6	339	8.4	287	7.5
Total £ area	464		632		605		508	
Austria	35	7.2	65	10.1	54	8.4	33	6.1
Sweden	110	9.4	202	10.8	196	11.3	137	8.7
Switzerland	79	7.5	117	8.5	96	7.9	71	6.0
Turkey	21	7.4	31	7.8	39	7.0	38	7.2
Total Continental EPU	245		415		385		279	
French OT's	103	6.1	179	7.6	200	7.5	235	6.5
Netherlands OT's	30	4.2	49	6.2	60	7.6	29	5.1
Portuguese OT's	10	7.2	13	7.9	16	8.3	13	6.8
Total non-£ EPU	388		656		661		556	
Colombia	18	5.0	21	5.2	23	5.4	27	5.4
El Salvador	3	6.1	4	6.6	4	6.5	5	6.6
Haiti	3	6.5	3	7.0	4	6.8	3	7.0
Mexico	18	3.5	29	3.8	25	3.4	25	3.2
Argentina	73	10.9	192	13.4	212	18.0	95	11.8
Chile	15	6.2	28	8.5	29	7.9	27	7.9
Uruguay	14	7.1	26	8.2	22	8.6	14	7.3
Total Latin America	144		303		319		196	
Finland	28	7.1	67	9.9	70	8.9	33	6.2
Yugoslavia	16	6.7	34	8.8	32	8.7	32	8.0
Spain	51	13.1	65	16.8	59	11.4	43 }	12.0
Spanish OT's	24	13.9	38	21.4	39	25.2	44 }	
Total other Europe	119		204		200		152	
Egypt	44	7.6	69	10.2	61	9.7	44	8.8
Iran	12	5.9	13	5.6	8	5.2	6	5.2
Israel	29	10.2	43	12.9	45	13.6	33	11.4
Lebanon	8	9	11	9	10	9	15	9
Syria	11	10	15	10	13	10	20	10
Saudi Arabia	8	10	15	10	22	10	17	10
Anglo-Egyptian Sudan	4	5.4	7	6.2	13	7.1	9	5.9
Total Middle East	116		173		172		144	
Indonesia	26	5.9	46	5.7	52	5.6	44	5.8
Taiwan	14	12	20	14	27	13	23	12
Thailand	19	9	25	9	27	9	30	9
South Korea	11	10	12	10	16	10	26	10
Total Far East	70		103		122		123	
Total other areas	305		480		494		419	
Total all areas	1,301		2,071		2,079		1,679	

Amounts include payments to domestic carriers.
Percentages without decimal figures are rough estimates.

Amplification of the Records

will in general be too high and the amounts of the U.S. and the U.K. too low. The same result, to a lesser extent, can be expected from the allocation by flag of carrier of freight on imported dry cargo transported en masse in tramp ships.

There are many obstacles to estimating the misallocation and arriving at a fairly accurate allocation of freight charges. First, the magnitude of the misallocation could be estimated only if we knew whether each carrier of commodities was operated by a resident of the country indicated by the ship's flag or of another country. This is particularly true of tramps. Of tankers not flying the flags of the U.K. or the U.S., there are good reasons to assume that they were chartered (although information is lacking on the proportion chartered by residents of those two countries). Because almost no countries show flag distributions of dry cargo vessels and tankers separately, a reallocation of the freight on imports of petroleum products was impossible. However, in the allocation of freight on imports by flag of carrier, shown below, the errors due to lack of information on chartering are, on the average, smaller than expected.

Secondly, few countries for which allocation of freight on imports had to be made show flag distributions of quantities of imported merchandise sufficiently detailed for that purpose. What is needed for accurate allocation is information about the nationality of carriers for every commodity (or group of commodities), for every route of transport, and by type of vessel (tramp or liner). With such detailed information and also the appropriate freight rates, in a few instances, allocation of freight on imports close to the actual could be made. For France, which publishes detailed flag distributions of its imports and exports, a description of the calculation and its results is given in Section 5.

A number of countries publish the flag distributions of total quantities of imported merchandise, and others show only the flag distributions of tonnages entering their ports. Both types of records were used here for allocation of freight on imports. A few countries—none important in transportation—show no flag distributions at all, and flag distributions of neighboring countries were used. The question remains, how reliable this yardstick of assorted records of flag distribution is for the allocation of the freight on imports.

A very detailed breakdown of freight on imports paid to foreign countries is given in the Danish balance of payments. A flag distribution of the unloaded quantities of merchandise as well as of the tonnages arrived at Danish ports is given in *Danish Ships and Shipping*.[14] Hence, for Denmark a comparison between the allocation of freight payments and the flag distribution of ships calling at its ports is given in Table 7.

[14] Published annually by the Statistical Department, Denmark.

Amplification of the Records

TABLE 7

COMPARISON OF ALLOCATION OF FREIGHT ON IMPORTS PAID BY DENMARK WITH FLAG DISTRIBUTION OF IMPORTED QUANTITIES AND OF VESSELS CALLING AT DANISH PORTS, 1951

Transporting Country	Allocation of Freight on Imports		Flag Distribution of Imports [a] Commodity Quantity		Carrying Tonnages	
DISTRIBUTION AMONG FOREIGN CARRIERS ONLY						
United Kingdom	9.5 [b]	12.5%	10.0 [c]	12.5%	5.7 [d]	10.4%
Rest of £ area	0.1	0.1	0.1	0.1	0.4	0.8
Total £ area	9.6	12.6	10.1	12.6	6.1	11.2
Norway	12.3	16.2	12.9	16.2	10.0	18.3
Sweden	12.7	16.7	13.4	16.8	13.7	25.1
West Germany	17.1	22.5	18.0	22.5	9.7	17.7
Netherlands	5.2	6.9	5.4	6.8	2.8	5.1
Belgium	0.1	0.1	0.1	0.1	0.1	0.2
France	1.1	1.5	1.2	1.5	0.6	1.1
Italy	0.6	0.8	0.7	0.9	0.3	0.5
Other OEEC	1.0	1.3	1.0	1.3	0.4	0.7
Total Continental OEEC	50.1	66.0	52.7	66.1	37.6	68.7
United States	9.0	11.9	9.5	11.9	6.1	11.1
Latin America	1.2	1.6	1.2	1.5	0.6	1.1
Finland	4.8	6.4	5.1	6.4	2.9	5.3
Poland	0.1	0.1	0.1	0.1	0.8	1.5
East Germany	0.1	0.1	0.1	0.1	0.1	0.2
Other East Europe	0.9	1.2	0.9	1.1	0.4	0.7
Total other Europe	5.9	7.8	6.2	7.7	4.2	7.7
Total other areas	0.1	0.1	0.2	0.2	0.1	0.2
Total foreign countries	75.9	100.0	79.9	100.0	54.7	100.0
DISTRIBUTION BETWEEN FOREIGN AND OWN CARRIERS						
Total foreign countries	75.9	76.2	79.9	66.7	54.7	58.0
Denmark	23.7	23.8	39.9	33.3	39.6	42.0
Grand total	99.6	100.0	119.8	100.0	94.3	100.0

[a] From *The Danish Merchant Marine and Shipping in 1951*, pp. 44 ff.
[b] Millions of U.S. dollars.
[c] Hundred thousand metric tons.
[d] Hundred thousand register tons.

Amplification of the Records

There appears to be an almost perfect correspondence between the allocation of freight on imports paid to foreigners and commodity quantities carried by foreign vessels. The flag distribution of the tonnages of foreign carriers deviates more than that of the imported quantities from the allocation of the freight payments. This is true of countries taken separately, but by areas the correspondence is much better and could be used to allocate the freight on imports in case the flag distribution of the imported quantities were not known.

Comparing the figures for total foreign countries and Denmark we see that the latter's share of the total freight on imports is smaller than its share of the tonnages that carried the imported commodities.[15] This is to be expected, since Denmark is the home country to which Danish vessels have to return, even without the average quantity of cargo. That Denmark's share of the freight on imports is smaller than its share in unloaded quantities of merchandise is explained by the preference of homebound Danish vessels for low freight quantities rather than empty holds. These points will be recalled in allocating total freight on imports of a country between foreign countries and the importing country itself.

It is worth noting that the average freight on imports paid to foreign carriers is about $9.50 per ton of cargo, and freight paid to foreign and domestic carriers together is about $8.30 per ton. The average c.i.f. value of cargo imported is $86.50 per ton, making Denmark's over-all share of freight in the c.i.f. value of imports approximately 9.6 per cent.

The correspondence between freight paid to foreign carriers and quantities transported by them, remarkably close for Denmark, leads to the question whether other countries might show as good correspondence. A comparison of the figures for Australia and Japan, both paying considerable amounts of freight on imports, is given in Table 8. In the Australian customs returns the imports are valued f.o.b. This suggests that most imported commodities are purchased f.o.b., and only slight adjustments had to be made in the exchange control records. Japan's customs returns record the c.i.f. value of imports. According to IMF *Yearbook,* however, import figures are changed to f.o.b. basis in a rather careful way, and the same probably applies to the area breakdown. For Australia, the 1951 allocation of total freight on imports is derived from the total payments on transportation after deducting $10 million from the sterling area (U.K.) and $15 million from nonsterling EPU [16] for estimated payments of passage fares, and the like. The freight on imports is compared with the flag distribution of the imported quantities of

---
[15] The tonnages that visited Danish ports in ballast are not included in the carrying tonnage figures.
[16] European Payments Union.

Amplification of the Records

TABLE 8
Comparison of Allocations of Freight on Imports with Flag Distribution of Imports, Australia 1951, Japan 1953

Transporting Country and Area	Australia 1951 Freight on Imports		Australia 1951 Flag Distribution of Imported Quantities		Japan 1953 Freight on Imports		Japan 1953 Flag Distribution of Imported Quantities	
United Kingdom	176 [a]	66.1%	81.9 [b]	62.7%			44.8 [c]	
Rest of £ area	7	3.0	3.4	2.6				
Total £ area	183	69.1	85.3	65.3	59.9	29.4%	44.8	29.2%
Norway			17.9				16.3	
Sweden			4.4				2.8	
Denmark			2.7 [d]				3.5	
Netherlands			5.4				6.8	
France			0.4 [d]				1.5	
Italy			1.1 [d]				7.8	
Greece							11.3	
Other OEEC								
Total continental OEEC	44	16.6	31.9	24.4	53.2	26.0	50.0	32.5
United States	11	4.1	4.0	3.1	36.3		18.3	
Canada	1	0.4			2.5		1.4	
Total North America	12	4.5	4.0	3.1	38.8	19.0	19.7	12.8
Panama			9.4 [b]				25.9 [c]	
Other Latin America								
Total Latin America	22 [a]	8.3	9.4	7.2	30.2	14.7	25.9	16.9
Far East					22.2		13.1	
Rest of world					0.1		0.1	
Total other areas	4	1.5			22.3	10.9	13.2	8.6
Total allocated	265	100.0	130.6	100.0	204.4	100.0	153.6	100.0
Unallocated			5.7		8.4		15.9	
Total foreign	265		136.3	99.2	212.8	62.5	169.5	54.0
Own country			1.1	0.8	130.0	37.5	143.3	46.0
Grand total	265		137.4 [e]	100.0	342.8	100.0	312.8	100.0

Source: For Australia, *Transport and Communication*, Commonwealth Bureau of Census and Statistics. The flag distribution is shown by fiscal year (weight and measurement combined). All figures are averages of 1950-51 and 1951-52. For Japan, *The Monthly Return of the Foreign Trade of Japan*, Ministry of Finance, Jan.-Dec., 1953, p. 425.

[a] Millions of U.S. dollars.
[b] Hundred thousand tons.
[c] Hundred thousand metric tons.
[d] Estimated on basis of tonnage entered.
[e] Equivalent to 10.694 million metric tons.

Amplification of the Records

merchandise in that year. For Japan, 1953, the least "abnormal" of all the years under study, was chosen as year of comparison.

For Australia, we see that the shares of the freight on imports of both the U.K. and the U.S. were higher than the shares of their vessels in the carriage of the imported quantities. The OEEC countries show the opposite relationship. This could be expected because of chartering but the differences do not detract from the general applicability of this yardstick.

For Japan, the results are the same with respect to the U.S.; its share of the freight paid on imports is greater than its share of the quantities imported by its carriers. The continental OEEC countries and Latin America (mainly Panama) show the opposite, again because of chartering of Continental European and Pan-American vessels by the U.S. for carrying part of its exports to Japan. The share of Japan in the total freight on imports is smaller than its share in imported quantities, for reasons given above to explain the same relationship for Denmark.

The average freight on imports paid to foreign carriers is about $27.10 (Australia, 1951) and $12.50 (Japan, 1953) per ton of cargo; and that paid

TABLE 9

FREIGHT ON IMPORTS STATED BUT UNALLOCATED
BY IMPORTING COUNTRY, 1950-1953
(millions of U.S. dollars)

Importing Country	1950	1951	1952	1953
Union of South Africa	81	117	118	115
Belgium	198	319	292	296
Italy	145	261	212	229
Netherlands	129	208	201	182
Norway	42	67	56	56
Total	514	855	761	763
Costa Rica	4	5	6	7
Dominican Republic	4	7	8	4
Nicaragua	4	5	7	7
Panama	8	8	10	10
Venezuela	71	87	95	95
Paraguay	4	5	8	6
Peru	33	48	37	38
Total	128	165	171	167
Grand total	723	1,137	1,050	1,045

Amplification of the Records

to foreign and domestic carriers together is about $27.10 and $11.60 per ton. The average c.i.f. value per ton of cargo imported is $188.10 and $177, so that the over-all share of the freight in the c.i.f. value of imports is approximately 14.4 per cent for Australia and 16.2 per cent for Japan.

Though the correspondence between the distributions is not so close for these two countries as for Denmark, the usefulness of the flag distribution for allocating the freight on imports appears to be established by these three comparisons. In case the importing country has a sizable fleet of its own, care must be used in estimating the share of freight on imports earned by its vessels, although earnings of such fleets are usually stated. The allocation of the freight on imports, estimated in this study, is shown in Appendix Table A-1.

Countries that estimated the freight on imports but did not allocate it to partner countries, are listed with their estimates in Table 9. Allocations of the freight on imports for these countries, on the basis of the flag distribution, are shown in Table A-2.

UNREPORTED SHIP EARNINGS AND DISBURSEMENTS

A serious understatement of total receipts as well as total payments on account of transportation was discussed in the part of Section 1 dealing with reported figures. The United Kingdom, for instance, does not report under transportation the receipts and payments of tankers operated by British oil companies. The revenues of these shipping activities are included in the financial outcome of all transactions of those oil companies and reported by the U.K. in the miscellaneous category. Clearly, this procedure causes an understatement of total receipts and payments in the world transportation account.

The earnings and disbursements of vessels flying the flags of Panama, Honduras, and Liberia are not reported at all by those countries, since they "do not consider the vessels as part of their economy" (IMF *Yearbook*). Among reasons for registering ships under those flags, an important one is that those countries do not demand financial statements showing either the total or foreign exchange earnings and expenditures of the ships flying their flags and do not levy taxes on the companies that own the ships. Another reason seems to be that those three countries do not keep a close watch on labor conditions prevailing on board those ships. These and other reasons explain the term "flags of convenience." Since Panama, Honduras, and Liberia are not informed about the finances of the vessels that fly their flags, they are unable to report receipts and disbursements in foreign exchange to the IMF.

The owners of ships flying the Greek flag are usually residents of other

Amplification of the Records

countries. The latter should report under transportation the earnings and disbursements of those ships according to the instructions in the *Manual*. Surpluses remitted to Greece should also be reported as investment income by Greece. It is safe to assume, however, that the earnings and disbursements of vessels flying the Greek flag are not included in the figures reported by those countries. This might be why Greece includes the amounts remitted to her in her transportation figures. Since only surpluses are remitted, it is clear that a large part of the earnings and disbursements of that fleet are not reported at all.

The ways in which these gaps in the transportation account have been filled are the subject of the next three subsections.

Tankers Operated by British Oil Companies [17]

Tanker operations affecting the balance of payments of the United Kingdom have been performed by two groups of companies: British oil companies like Anglo Iranian and Royal Dutch Shell; British subsidiaries of American companies, which sell for sterling, on behalf of the parent companies, petroleum products to various countries of the sterling area. Since those subsidiaries are residents of the U.K. the outcome of their transactions should also be reported by the U.K., according to the instructions in the IMF *Manual*. However, the receipts as well as the disbursements abroad for the transportation of petroleum had to be estimated for both groups of companies.

The way in which the amounts to be put on the credit and debit sides of the U.K. transportation account were estimated is essentially the same as that to be used later for estimating credits and debits for transportation of dry cargo, discussed in the fifth section. The idea is more simple than the means for carrying it out. It amounts essentially to a reconstruction of the freight bill by making use of the quantities moved in world trade and the corresponding freight rates.

Dwyer had a good idea of the quantities of petroleum products imported by each country from various sources in 1951, and he could determine the shares that British and American oil companies had in the supply of petroleum that year. The freight rates charged by those companies for the carriage of petroleum products along each route were available. They are based on the so-called London Award, a time charter rate expressed in shillings per deadweight [18] ton (DWT) per month for

[17] In preparing this section I benefited from the MS. study of Cornelius J. Dwyer, "The Oil Trade in the International Balance of Payments in 1951," National Bureau of Economic Research, December 1955, p. 5. Table 17 of that paper shows a world freight bill for tankers, allocated to the countries that were engaged in the transportation of petroleum products.
[18] Weight of the ship without cargo.

Amplification of the Records

a tanker with standard speed. The time rates were converted in this study into voyage rates by taking into account the average number of miles that can be traversed by such a standard tanker, after allowing for "nonproductivity" because of loading and unloading, minor repairs, and so on.

By multiplying the quantities moved along each route by the appropriate freight rates, the tanker freight bill of 1951 was reconstructed for the world as a whole, and also for the shares that British and American oil companies, in particular their subsidiaries in the U.K., had in it. To arrive at the amounts to be put on the credit side of the U.K. 1951 transportation account, earnings of tankers operated by subsidiaries of British oil companies in France, the Netherlands, and other countries were subtracted. The allocation of the total amounts to the U.K. and to foreign countries is shown in Table A-3.

To determine how much was paid by British and American oil companies located in the U.K. for charter hire to foreign countries, information on the ownership of tankers in operation during 1951 was obtained from a publication of the Supply and Transportation Division of the Petroleum Administration for Defense (PAD), *World Tank Ship Fleet Balances 1950-1952*.[19] The deadweight tonnage, at standard (T-2) speed, owned by oil companies (American and British) as well as by non-oil companies and governments, by flag of vessel as of April 1, 1951, is shown in Table 15 of that publication. The table was brought into line with the tonnage actually in use on July 1, 1951, as shown in the statistical appendix of *Lloyd's Register of Shipping*.

All tankers owned and chartered were assumed to be fully employed in 1951, and of the total tonnage operated by oil companies located in the U.K. the part chartered to them was determined. The next step was to decide what proportion British "free market" tankers had in the total tonnage chartered, since the charter fee paid for those tankers does not affect the U.K.'s balance of payments. The remaining part of the chartered tonnage has been charged with the full charter hire, discussed in the next subsection. Meanwhile, what is meant here by charter hire includes all costs, charter fee as well as operating expenses, in so far as they are paid by the charterer. For tankers chartered from foreign countries, it can be assumed that all those costs are paid in foreign exchange and belong on the debit side of the transportation account of the U.K. They have been allocated mainly to nonsterling EPU countries (Norway, Sweden, Denmark, and others).

[19] Additional information on some of the tables in this publication was supplied to us by Mr. Cross and Mr. Hunter McDowell of the Statistical Research Division of the Sun Oil Company (Philadelphia, Pennsylvania). That company continues the work started at PAD and issues every year *Analysis of World Tank Ship Fleets*, which contains many interesting details on tankers all over the world.

Amplification of the Records

As for the "free market" tankers under the United Kingdom's flag chartered to British oil companies, only the costs over and above the charter fee, in so far as they are paid by the charterer, have affected the U.K.'s balance of payments. In general these additional costs consist of port expenditures, canal tolls, and so on. Fuel is usually a cost to the charterer but is not counted here, because it may be assumed that the oil companies did not pay for the fuel consumed by the tankers they operated.

The part of operating expenses of tankers owned by British oil companies, presumably paid in foreign exchange, had to be estimated. It consists of costs enumerated above for chartered British tankers plus ships' stores and repair costs. Wages are not counted for the British oil company tankers, because it can be assumed that their crews are predominantly British and paid in British currency.

The costs in excess of charter hire for chartered tankers, and the operating expenses for owned tankers were estimated on the basis of average costs per DWT, discussed more fully in the next subsection. The total computed amounts of additional costs were allocated in correspondence with the freight receipts; the breakdown is given in Table A-3.

The freight earnings of British oil companies in 1952 were computed in almost the same way as those for 1951, with only one difference—the computations were based on the number of ton miles actually produced in 1952, rather than on the exported and imported quantities. Multiplying the ton miles by an average freight (approximately $2.20 per 1,000 ton miles) yielded the freight amounts charged by British oil companies in 1952 for transportation of petroleum products in the tankers they operated. The average freight was found by weighting the 1952 Caribbean–United Kingdom and Middle East–United Kingdom freight rates per ton mile. Use of an average freight rate instead of a freight rate for every route makes the 1952 computation to a certain extent less exact than the 1951 calculation, but accurate enough in this phase of the study.

To assess the amount paid by British oil companies for 1952 charter hire, use was made of the same (adjusted) PAD table used for 1951. Since the increase in tonnage used from mid-1951 to mid-1952 was not the same for all countries, the proportions were not the same as for the year 1951; but the correction to be made because of these changes is minor.

The freight earnings of tankers operated by British oil companies in 1950 and 1953 could not be computed in the same way as for 1951 and 1952, since there was no detailed information available on quantities moved or ton miles produced. The more over-all computations are based on average increases in the transported quantities of approximately 5

Amplification of the Records

per cent from 1950 to 1951 and 5 per cent from 1952 to 1953. By taking account of an increase in freight rates per ton mile of 60 per cent from 1950 to 1951, and a decrease of 38 per cent from 1952 to 1953, the amounts earned in those years by tankers operated by British oil companies were calculated. For the charter hire paid to foreign countries the proportions found for 1951 were used for 1950 and 1953 to obtain the less accurate figures.

Despite these shortcomings in the 1950 and 1953 computations, it can still be claimed that the computations here of both the receipts and payments of foreign exchange by the United Kingdom for tanker operations are more accurate than ever before, particularly those for 1951 and 1952.

Ships under the Flags of Convenience

In estimating the freight earnings and disbursements of vessels flying the flags of Panama, Honduras, and Liberia it was clear that four categories of vessels had to be distinguished: the first distinction was between tankers and dry cargo vessels, since average earnings and disbursements of these two types of vessels are quite different; for the same reason, each of these two types of vessels was divided into two categories —vessels operated on voyage charter by their owners, and vessels let on time charter to foreigners. The receipts and payments of each of these four categories of ships were estimated separately for each of the four years under study.

With almost nothing known about the operation of ships flying the flags of Panama, Honduras, and Liberia, a search was undertaken for information on ships that, from an operational standpoint, could be compared with ships under the flags of convenience. Some Scandinavian publications supply a wealth of information on the performance of such ships, particularly for Norway. But the applicability of Norwegian averages to the operation of the fleets under study is immediately open to question.

On the disbursement side, there is the contention that the running expenses of ships under the flags of convenience are much lower because of the loose supervision of labor conditions prevailing on board. However, wages constitute in general no more than about 15 per cent of all running expenses of the comparable ships dealt with in Scandinavian publications. Hence, the small difference in cost casts doubt upon savings in wages as the principal reason for registering ships under those flags, even in such a competitive trade as international shipping. Rather, the main reason for the transfer must be sought in avoiding taxes, which are really excessive in some countries and the subject of many com-

Amplification of the Records

plaints.[20] A more important fact is that part of the Norwegian ship running expenses are not paid in foreign exchange—are not disbursements abroad. At this point the Norwegian averages had to be supplemented by use of Danish statistics, explained later.

On the earnings side, Norwegian averages are probably more applicable than on the disbursement side, since there is strong similarity between the operation of Norwegian ships and of ships under the flags of convenience. In both instances only a small percentage of revenues is obtained from the carriage of imports and exports of the flag's country, and almost all earnings stem from transporting commodities between foreign countries. The ships wander about for long stretches of time, visiting one foreign country after another, and return only occasionally to their home countries. It is on the basis of these and similar considerations that Norwegian averages are used for estimating the disbursements as well as the earnings of the fleets in question.

A rich source of information on the performance of Norwegian ships in the years under study is *Norske Skip I Utenriksfart,* probably unequaled by any other source in the field of international shipping activities. It supplied the information on the previously mentioned four categories of ships used here as a basis for computing the earnings and disbursements of the Pan. Hon. Lib. fleet. Some of the relevant 1953 figures were estimated in advance of their appearance. This basic material is shown in Table 10.

The tonnage figures given by *Lloyd's Register* for tankers in 1950 and 1951 refer to ships of 1,000 GRT and over. In order to convert all *Lloyd's* figures to that basis, the tanker figures for 1952 and 1953 were increased by 60,000 GRT, a figure derived from *Norske Skip,* Table r, giving the tonnages of ships in various size groups. The end-of-year tonnages of the dry cargo and passenger fleet were obtained by subtracting the tanker tonnages from the total fleet tonnages. *Norske Skip* does not give the dry cargo fleet tonnages separately, and consequently the relevant figures of Table 10 are estimated. The difference between the two figures stated for tankers and dry cargo ships at the end of each year is due, first to a difference in cut-off point (25 versus 500 GRT) and, secondly, to the difference in the tonnages in domestic trade.

Allowance was made in the figures for average tonnages in foreign trade during each year for ships out of service for at least eleven months

---

[20] A good description of the many and heavy taxes levied on Norwegian ship owners is given by Kaare Petersen on pages 19-21 of the ten-year anniversary issue of *Norwegian Shipping News.* The connection betweeen taxes and transfer to flags of convenience is also discussed at length in the 1955 annual report of the Chamber of Shipping of the United Kingdom.

TABLE 10

NORWEGIAN TONNAGES, RECEIPTS AND PAYMENTS FOR INTERNATIONAL SHIPPING ACTIVITIES, 1949-1953
(tonnages in 1,000 GRT; receipts and payments in millions of U.S. dollars)

	1949	1950	1951	1952	1953
		FLEET			
Tonnages					
1. End of year	5,300	5,681	5,975	6,249	6,500 [a]
2. July 1 of year		5,557	5,817	5,907	6,264
		TANKER FLEET			
1. End of year	2,272	2,631	2,990	3,245	3,450 [a]
2. July 1 of year		2,547 [b]	2,959 [b]	3,076	3,362
3. In foreign trade, end of year	2,045	2,395	2,753	3,066	3,140 [a]
4. In foreign trade, during year [c]		2,110	2,535	2,882	2,950 [a]
4. On voyage charter		593	732	796	830 [a]
4. On time charter		1,517	1,803	2,086	2,120 [a]
Voyage Receipts and Payments					
5. Freight receipts		44.1	109.7	121.1	93.5
6. Payments abroad		19.8	33.3	39.3	37.1
Total payments		26.3 [b]	45.0 [b]	51.5 [b]	54.8 [b]
Time Receipts and Payments					
5. Freight receipts		79.9	99.5	115.6	125.6
6. Payments abroad		26.3	30.0	36.0	40.6
Total payments		47.5 [b]	52.3 [b]	60.0 [b]	74.1 [b]
	DRY CARGO AND PASSENGER FLEET				
Tonnages					
1. End of year	3,028	3,050	2,985	3,004	3,050 [a]
2. July 1 of year		2,910	2,858	2,831	2,902
		DRY CARGO FLEET			
1. End of year	2,880 [a]	2,900 [a]	2,835 [a]	2,855 [a]	2,900 [a]
3. In foreign trade, end of year	2,392	2,430	2,362	2,287	2,410 [a]
4. In foreign trade, during year		2,347	2,357	2,285	2,290 [a]
4. On voyage charter		1,581	1,623	1,529	1,545 [a]
4. On time charter		766	734	756	745 [a]
Voyage Receipts and Payments					
5. Freight receipts		182.0	273.0	253.0	216.5
6. Payments abroad		108.4	138.9	142.2	131.1
Total payments		143.7 [b]	187.0 [b]	182.7 [b]	174.7 [b]
Time Receipts and Payments					
5. Freight receipts		46.1	60.2	72.8	57.7
6. Payments abroad		19.0	22.0	27.0	23.8
Total payments		34.8 [b]	42.5 [b]	46.9 [b]	45.7 [b]

SOURCE BY LINE

1. *Norske Skip*, table a, vessels of 25 GRT and over.
2. *Lloyds's Register*, Appendix section 6 or 7, vessels of 100 GRT and over.
3. *Norske Skip*, table c, vessels of 500 GRT and over.
4. *Norske Skip*, table d.
5. *Norske Skip*, table n.
6. *Norske Skip*, table q.

[a] Estimated.
[b] Adjusted.
[c] 1,000 GRT on the average.

Amplification of the Records

per year, and for new ships for the months not yet in operation. From the stated figures the average earnings per GRT of both tankers and dry cargo ships on active duty, on voyage and on time charter can be computed.

The disbursement figures of *Norske Skip* refer only to expenditures outside Norway and do not include payments in domestic currency. Since the Pan. Hon. Lib. fleet has actually no home country, all its expenditures and receipts are in foreign exchange and should be recorded in its balance of payments. In order to serve as a basis for the Pan. Hon. Lib. fleet, the Norwegian disbursements (*Norske Skip*) were, therefore, increased to include also the payments in Norway. The figures used for the increases were for activities of the Danish merchant marine in those years, from *Skibsfarts-beretning for Året, 1954*. The revenues and running expenses, in foreign and domestic currency of the fourteen largest companies operating tankers, tramps, and liners, comprising 65 per cent of the Danish merchant fleet, are given for 1948 and following years (page 137). The proportions between average earnings and average disbursements of the Danish fleet were used to obtain gross figures for Norwegian disbursements to serve as a basis for the Pan. Hon. Lib. fleet.

The only information available on tonnages for the latter is contained in *Lloyd's Register*, giving the number of tons of the entire fleet and of tankers, July 1 of each year. The computation of receipts and payments was therefore based upon the tonnages given by *Lloyd's* for Norway, as shown in Table 11.

The tonnages of tankers and dry cargo ships exceeding 500 GRT were taken from those exceeding 25 GRT (Table r of *Norske Skip*). The percentages of ships in foreign trade, July 1 of each year, were more or less assumed on the basis of percentages given for the beginning and the end of the year. The percentages of ships on voyage and on time charter are the same as those in Table 10.

The composition of the fleets carrying the flags of Panama, Honduras, and Liberia in the four years of the study, taken from *Lloyd's Register*, are shown in Table 12. The tanker figures for 1950 and 1951 were corrected for the difference in cut-off points as in the case of Norway; the dry cargo figures were corrected accordingly.

In relating tonnages of ships carrying flags of convenience to those of Norwegian ships to estimate the receipts as well as the disbursements of the Pan. Hon. Lib. fleet, differences in average speeds of the two fleets were taken into account. For, the higher the speed the better the performance, which means generally higher earnings as well as disbursements per GRT. The differences in average speed of tankers appear in Table 13.

Amplification of the Records

TABLE 11

Tonnages, Receipts and Payments of Norwegian Ships, 1949-1953
(tonnages in 1,000 GRT; receipts and payments in millions of U.S. dollars)

Tonnages	1949	1950	1951	1952	1953
TANKERS					
1. Exceeding 25 GRT, end of year	2,272	2,631	2,990	3,245	3,450 [a]
2. Exceeding 500 GRT, end of year	2,192 [a]	2,546 [a]	2,900 [a]	3,150 [a]	3,350 [a]
3. In foreign trade, end of year	2,045	2,395	2,753	3,066	3,140 [a]
Per cent of (2)	93.3	94.0	94.9	97.3	94.3
4. Exceeding 100 GRT, July 1 of year		2,547 [b]	2,959 [b]	3,076	3,362
5. In foreign trade, July 1 of year		2,395	2,810	2,955	3,160
Per cent of (4)		94	95	96	94
6. On voyage charter, July 1 of year		675	810	815	885
Per cent of (5)		28.1	28.9	27.6	28.1
Receipts		44.1	109.7	121.1	93.5
Payments		26.3	45.0	51.5	54.8
7. On time charter, July 1 of year		1,720	2,000	2,140	2,275
Per cent of (5)		71.9	71.1	72.4	71.9
Receipts		79.9	99.5	115.6	125.6
Payments		47.5	52.3	60.0	74.1
DRY CARGO SHIPS					
8. Exceeding 25 GRT, end of year	2,880 [a]	2,900 [a]	2,835 [a]	2,855 [a]	2,900 [a]
9. Exceeding 500 GRT, end of year	2,510 [a]	2,530 [a]	2,465 [a]	2,485 [a]	2,530 [a]
10. In foreign trade, end of year	2,392	2,430	2,362	2,287	2,410 [a]
Per cent of (9)	95.3	96.1	95.8	92.0	95.3
11. Exceeding 100 GRT, July 1 of year		2,775	2,725	2,695	2,765
12. In foreign trade, July 1 of year		2,665	2,615	2,535	2,625
Per cent of (11)		96	96	94	95
13. On voyage charter, July 1 of year		1,795	1,800	1,695	1,770
Per cent of (12)		67.4	68.9	66.9	67.5
Receipts		182.0	273.0	253.0	216.5
Payments		143.7	187.0	182.7	174.7
14. On time charter, July 1 of year		870	815	840	855
Per cent of (12)		32.6	31.1	33.1	32.5
Receipts		46.1	60.2	72.8	57.7
Payments		34.8	42.5	46.9	45.7

[a] Estimated.
[b] Adjusted.

Amplification of the Records

TABLE 12

DISTRIBUTION OF FLEETS UNDER FLAGS OF CONVENIENCE, JULY 1 OF 1950-1953
(in 1,000 GRT)

	1950	1951	1952	1953
All Ships				
Panama	3,370	3,618	3,749	3,915
Honduras	523	508	468	471
Liberia	245	595	898	1,434
Total	4,138	4,721	5,115	5,820
Tankers				
Panama	1,740	1,765	1,843	2,151
Honduras	162	148	147	135
Liberia	230	432	608	1,029
Total	2,132	2,345	2,598	3,315
Correction	+50	+50		
Total	2,182	2,395		
Dry Cargo Ships				
Panama	1,630	1,853	1,906	1,764
Honduras	361	360	321	336
Liberia	15	163	290	405
Total	2,006	2,376	2,517	2,505
Correction	−50	−50		
Total	1,956	2,326		

TABLE 13

AVERAGE SPEED OF TANKERS, SELECTED DATES, 1951-1953
(knots)

	April 1, 1951 [a]		Oct. 1, 1952 [b]		Dec. 31, 1953 [c]	
Tankers	DWT [d]	Average speed	DWT [d]	Average speed	DWT [d]	Average speed
Panama	2,696.2	14.0	2,946.0	13.6	3,457.0	13.8
Honduras	238.8	14.6	229.5	14.2	220.7	14.4
Liberia	672.7	15.3	1,087.6	14.8	2,037.9	15.0
Total	3,607.7	14.3	4,263.1	14.0	5,715.6	14.3
Norway	4,040.5	12.9	4,767.1	13.2	5,389.6	13.3

[a] *World Tank Ship Fleet Balances*, PAD, 1950-1952, Table 14.
[b] *Analysis of World Tank Ship Fleet*, Sun Oil Company, October 1, 1952, Table 9.
[c] *Ibid.*, December 31, 1953, Table 11.
[d] Dead weight ton (see text footnote 18).

Amplification of the Records

It appears from these figures that there was a 5 to 10 per cent difference in the average speed of the Norwegian and the Pan. Hon. Lib. tanker fleets in those years. The average speed of dry cargo ships is, however, not readily available and would have to be computed to enable a similar comparison. But even if we knew the average speeds, there still remains the question how this would affect receipts and expenditures. There is no straight relationship between average speed and average earnings and disbursements, not even under the assumption of full employment. Because of these considerations, no correction was made in the Norwegian earnings and expenditures per GRT for differences in average speed of the ships. While no correction was made in those figures for the Pan. Hon. Lib. fleet for ships not in active service during these years, such a correction was made for Norway. This might to a certain extent compensate for the effect of disregarding the differences in average speed of both fleets.

A distinction has been made, however, between both the Pan. Hon. Lib. tankers and dry cargo ships according to their operation on voyage or on time charter. Essentially, the Norwegian proportions have been assumed, though some modification proved to be necessary for tankers. As Table 14 shows, a large share of the Pan. Hon. Lib. tanker tonnage, but only a negligible share of Norwegian tanker tonnage, was owned by oil companies or their subsidiaries.

To separate the Pan. Hon. Lib. ships operated on voyage charter and on time charter, it was assumed that the tankers owned by oil companies

TABLE 14

Proportionate Share of Tankers Owned by Oil Companies, Selected Dates, 1951-1953
(in T-2 units [a])

	April 1, 1951 [b]			October 1, 1952 [c]			December 31, 1953 [d]		
	All Tankers	Oil Co.	%	All Tankers	Oil Co.	%	All Tankers	Oil Co.	%
Panama	155.3	78.4	50.5	165.3	70.3	42.5	196.9	68.2	34.6
Honduras	14.4	–	–	13.4	–	–	13.1	–	–
Liberia	42.3	11.0	26.0	66.2	13.8	20.8	125.9	30.5	24.2
Total	212.0	89.4	42.2	244.9	84.1	34.3	335.9	98.7	29.4
Norway	213.7	5.4	2.5	258.3	5.1	2.0	293.9	5.7	1.9

[a] T-2 is a standard type tanker of 16,765 DWT with a speed of 14.5 knots.
[b] *World Tank Ship Fleet Balances*, 1950-1952, Table 15.
[c] *Analysis of World Tank Ship Fleet*, Table 10.
[d] *Ibid.*, Table 12.

Amplification of the Records

or their subsidiaries were operated on voyage charter. For the remaining part of the Pan. Hon. Lib. fleet, the Norwegian proportions were assumed to apply. Table 15 shows the results of that distinction between tonnages on voyage and on time charter.

TABLE 15

TONNAGES OF FLEETS CARRYING FLAGS OF PANAMA, HONDURAS, AND LIBERIA OPERATED ON VOYAGE AND ON TIME CHARTER, 1950-1953
(tonnages in 1,000 GRT)

	1950	1951	1952	1953
Tankers				
Total fleet	2,182	2,395	2,598	3,315
Owned by oil companies (%)	47.5	41.0	35.5	31.0
Owned by oil companies	1,036	982	922	1,028
Tons remaining	1,146	1,413	1,676	2,287
On voyage charter (%)	28.7	29.5	28.2	28.7
On voyage charter	329	417	473	656
Owned by oil companies	1,036	982	922	1,028
Total on voyage charter	1,365	1,399	1,395	1,684
Total on time charter	817	996	1,203	1,631
Dry Cargo Ships				
Total fleet	1,956	2,326	2,517	2,505
On voyage charter (%)	67.4	68.9	66.9	67.5
On voyage charter	1,318	1,603	1,684	1,691
On time charter	638	723	833	814

The average proportionate shares of tankers owned by oil companies in each year were obtained by linear interpolation. In fixing the percentages of tankers not owned by oil companies and operated on voyage charter, due account was taken of the small proportion of the Norwegian fleet that is owned by oil companies.

With the figures of Tables 11 and 15, the receipts and payments of the Pan. Hon. Lib. fleet could be estimated, as shown in Table 16.

The receipts of gross freight from voyage charters were allocated according to the freight payments to the Pan. Hon. Lib. fleet. The receipts of charter hire from the United States are the Department of Commerce amounts for payments of charter hire to the Pan. Hon. Lib. fleet. The remaining charter hire receipts are equally spread over the United Kingdom and the nonsterling EPU countries. The disbursements under both voyage and time charter are allocated according to the receipts of freight and charter hire. The specification can be found in Table A-4.

Amplification of the Records

TABLE 16

ESTIMATED RECEIPTS AND PAYMENTS OF FLEETS CARRYING FLAGS
OF PANAMA, HONDURAS, AND LIBERIA, 1950-1953
(tonnages in 1,000 GRT; amounts in millions of U.S. dollars)

	1950	1951	1952	1953
Tankers				
On voyage charter				
Norway				
Tonnage	675	810	815	885
Receipts	44.1	109.7	121.1	93.5
Payments	26.3	45.0	51.5	54.8
Pan. Hon. Lib.				
Tonnage	1,365	1,399	1,395	1,684
Receipts	85.1	181.5	207.3	177.9
Payments	50.8	74.4	88.1	104.3
On time charter				
Norway				
Tonnage	1,720	2,000	2,140	2,275
Receipts	79.9	99.5	115.6	125.6
Payments	47.5	52.3	60.0	74.1
Pan. Hon. Lib.				
Tonnage	817	996	1,203	1,631
Receipts	36.2	47.5	65.0	90.0
Payments	21.5	25.0	33.7	53.1
Dry Cargo Ships				
On voyage charter				
Norway				
Tonnage	1,795	1,800	1,695	1,770
Receipts	182.0	273.0	253.0	216.5
Payments	143.7	187.0	182.7	174.7
Pan. Hon. Lib.				
Tonnage	1,318	1,603	1,684	1,691
Receipts	133.6	243.1	251.4	206.8
Payments	105.5	166.5	181.5	166.9
On time charter				
Norway				
Tonnage	870	815	840	855
Receipts	46.1	60.2	72.8	57.7
Payments	34.8	42.5	46.9	45.7
Pan. Hon. Lib.				
Tonnage	638	723	833	814
Receipts	33.8	53.4	72.2	54.9
Payments	25.5	37.7	46.5	43.5

Amplification of the Records

What is needed in the balance of payments figures is a special column for payments to the Pan. Hon. Lib. fleet in the area breakdown. This would provide a check on the total earnings of the vessels flying those flags as well as of the regional distribution of these earnings. Therefore, in the Appendix tables a column has been introduced for payments to these fleets as a first attempt at providing such a check.

The Greek Fleet

With the detailed description in mind of how the receipts and expenditures of the Pan. Hon. Lib. fleet have been estimated, the discussion of estimates for the Greek fleet will be brief. As for the proportion of tonnages operated on voyage and on time charter, the Norwegian percentages have been used without modification. Table 17 shows the re-

TABLE 17

TONNAGES OF THE GREEK FLEET OPERATED ON VOYAGE CHARTER
AND ON TIME CHARTER, 1950-1953
(tonnages in 1,000 GRT)

	1950	1951	1952	1953
All vessels	1,349	1,277	1,274	1,222
Tankers	102	104	111	121
Corrected	105	107	111	121
On voyage charter (%)	28.1	28.9	27.6	28.1
On voyage charter	30	31	31	34
On time charter	75	76	80	87
Dry cargo ships	1,244	1,170	1,163	1,101
On voyage charter (%)	67.4	68.9	66.9	67.5
On voyage charter	838	806	778	743
On time charter	406	364	385	358

sults. Relating these figures to those of Norway (Table 11) yielded the estimated earnings and disbursements of the Greek fleet, shown in Table 18.

It appears from this comparison that the reported net receipts are in all four years smaller than the calculated net earnings, particularly in 1951 and 1952, the years of excessively high freight rates. This could mean that the net receipts as reported include only amortization and interest on capital invested in the fleet, but exclude profits made by the owners of the ships. The difference between the calculated gross earnings and the reported net receipts has been put on the receipts side

TABLE 18

ESTIMATED RECEIPTS AND PAYMENTS OF GREEK FLEET, 1950-1953
(tonnages in GRT; amounts in millions of U.S. dollars)

	1950	1951	1952	1953
Tankers				
On voyage charter				
Norway				
Tonnage	675	810	815	885
Receipts	44.1	109.7	121.1	93.5
Payments	26.3	45.0	51.5	54.8
Greece				
Tonnage	29	31	31	34
Receipts	1.9	4.2	4.6	3.6
Payments	1.1	1.7	1.9	2.1
On time charter				
Norway				
Tonnage	1,720	2,000	2,140	2,275
Receipts	79.9	99.5	115.6	125.6
Payments	47.5	52.3	60.0	74.1
Greece				
Tonnage	76	76	80	87
Receipts	3.5	3.8	3.8	4.8
Payments	1.9	2.0	2.0	2.8
Dry Cargo Ships				
On voyage charter				
Norway				
Tonnage	1,795	1,800	1,695	1,770
Receipts	182.0	273.0	253.0	216.5
Payments	143.7	187.0	182.7	174.7
Greece				
Tonnage	838	806	778	743
Receipts	85.0	122.3	116.1	90.9
Payments	67.1	83.8	83.9	73.4
On time charter				
Norway				
Tonnage	870	815	840	855
Receipts	46.1	60.2	72.8	57.7
Payments	34.8	42.5	46.9	45.7
Greece				
Tonnage	406	364	385	358
Receipts	21.5	26.9	33.3	24.2
Payments	16.3	19.0	21.5	19.1

COMPARISON: ESTIMATED EARNINGS AND EXPENSES WITH NET RECEIPTS
REPORTED BY GREECE

	1950	1951	1952	1953
Reported				
Total receipts	23	31	36	27
Sales of ship stores, etc.	3	4	2	1
Net receipts	20	27	34	26
Estimated				
Total receipts	112	157	158	124
Running expenses	86	107	110	97
Net receipts	26	50	48	27

Amplification of the Records

and the calculated running expenses on the payments side of Greece's transportation account. No reduction was made for freight on imports earned by Greek ships, since it is clearly stated in the IMF *Yearbook* that these freight earnings have not been deducted from the estimated total freight on imports. The allocation of freight earnings and of expenditures, in conformity with that of Norway (*Norske Skip I Utenriksfart*), is shown in Table A-5.

MISCELLANEOUS

Receipts from Sales of Fuel Out of Bunkers

The payments for bunker fuel, part of the running expenses of the carriers, are reported on the debit side of the transportation accounts of the countries that own the ships. Accordingly, the receipts from sales of fuel out of bunkers should be recorded on the credit side of the transportation accounts of the receiving countries. However, a number of countries fail to follow this practice.

Some countries—for instance, the Canary Islands—include sales of fuel out of bunkers under their merchandise exports; the amounts involved were deducted here from merchandise and entered into the transportation account of that country. Another necessary correction was for the United Kingdom, which reports receipts from sale of fuel out of bunkers, like those from all petroleum transactions, under Miscellaneous. Still other countries are on a special trade basis and consequently do not include the amount of fuel, going into and coming from bonded warehouses, in their payments for merchandise and receipts from transportation. A number, particularly the overseas territories of European countries, do not report receipts from sales of fuel out of bunkers at all.

The amounts involved were calculated on the basis of quantities supplied by each country and estimated average prices charged for it.[21] Separate calculations were made for oil and coal, the latter being of minor importance in this respect. An average price for fuel oil supplied by each country was estimated and multiplied by the relevant quantities, resulting in the figures shown in Table A-6. The same procedure was followed for estimating receipts from sales of coal out of bunkers, using different sources of information. The quantities were derived from the

[21] The quantities of oil supplied in 1950 and 1951 were derived from official U.N. publications (for 1950, Statistical Papers, Series J, No. 1, pages 81-83; for 1953, *Monthly Bulletin of Statistics*, March 1955, page xv). The information on the quantities of oil supplied out of bunkers in 1951 and 1952 was kindly supplied by N. B. Guyol, Chief of the Industrial Statistics Section of the Economic Statistics Branch of the United Nations.

The prices of oil out of bunkers were obtained from *Marine Fuel Oils*, Esso Export Corporation, stating prices for different sorts of fuel oil supplied by the most important bunkering stations.

Amplification of the Records

official publication, *Statistical Summary of the Mineral Industry* (London, 1955). The average prices were estimated on the basis of prices charged for the supply of coal by the country in question.

The next step was to determine how much of those amounts was received by domestic carriers, leaving the rest to be credited on the country's transportation account. Some countries, like the Netherlands, show in their foreign trade statistics how much was taken in by their own carriers, but for most countries the amounts had to be estimated. For each country, the estimates were based on the tonnages of ships under various flags that entered the ports of the country with cargo or in ballast. The same yardstick was used to determine how much each foreign area contributed to the receipts on account of fuel deliveries. The results are shown in Table A-5.

Since practically all the bunker fuel has been supplied by British or American oil companies, it might be that countries owning vessels allocated the payments to the U.K. and the U.S. rather than to the countries where the fuel was taken in. Since the principle of country-of-origin rather than country-of-sale was followed here in dealing with oil, it is possible that the allocation to a country of payments for bunker fuel does not match the allocation of the total amounts received from it.

Port Receipts

Apart from receipts from sale of bunker fuel there are two other kinds of port receipts. The first group consists of harbor dues, light dues, dues for anchorage or mooring, berth dues or wharfage, pilotage and towage. All these charges are related to the ship that visits the port and are usually quoted in a certain amount per net register ton (NRT), sometimes per GRT. The second group of port receipts is related to the cargo delivered and loaded in port and consists of loading and unloading charges, stevedorage, and so forth. The amounts involved are usually higher than those of the first group of dues.

There is a question whether the amounts charged for loading and unloading cargo should be included in the port receipts of the exporting and importing country's balance of payments. According to the instructions given in the *Manual*, exports and imports should be evaluated f.o.b., which means that in this system of recording the loading charges should be included in the price of the merchandise. What has been stipulated in the purchase contract with respect to the loading and unloading charges, therefore, determines whether they will or will not appear on the transportation line of the given countries' records.

Let us assume, for example, that the price of a commodity before loading is 90 money units, the loading charges 2, the freight 6, and the unloading charges also 2 money units. There are four different ways in

Amplification of the Records

which these charges can be settled, for the two extremes of which the entries as required by the *Manual* are:

1. The loading charge is paid by the exporter to a stevedore in his country, and the unloading charge is paid by the importer in his country; the entries in the balance of payments of the country of export (X), of transport (Y) and of import (Z) are then as follows:

	X		Y		Z	
	C	D	C	D	C	D
Merchandise	92					92
Transportation			6			6

2. The loading and unloading charges are first paid by the carrier and then passed on to the importer; the entries are now:

	X		Y		Z	
	C	D	C	D	C	D
Merchandise	90					90
Transportation (from Y)	2		(from Z) 4	(to X) 2		
				(to Z) 2		
			(from Z) 6		(from Y) 2	(to Y) 4
						(to Y) 6

The last method is most common, and consequently the amount paid to the carrier is assumed always to include the loading and unloading charges.

The dues related to the ship (first group, above) can be found in publications like *Ports of the World*,[22] which give sometimes also particulars about stevedorage. More information on the latter can be found in publications of the Baltic and International Maritime Conference (main office, Copenhagen). Both give specific details on the various kinds of costs ships of different sizes must pay for harbor and other dues, and for loading or unloading particular types of cargo in specific ports.

Rather than using this detailed information for estimating the port receipts of particular countries, the estimates here are based on information of a much more general character. Some countries—for instance, Italy and Japan—give a careful account of their port receipts, information on the tonnage under foreign flags visiting their ports, and also on quantities of cargo delivered and loaded by foreign ships. The figures are shown in Table 19.

[22] *Ports of the World*, 5th Ed., Archibald Hurd and Paul E. Chevalier, eds., London, 1951.

Amplification of the Records

TABLE 19

PORT RECEIPTS, TONNAGES ENTERED, AND CARGO DELIVERED AND LOADED, ITALY AND JAPAN, 1950-1953

	1950	1951	1952	1953
Italy				
Port receipts ($ mil.)	$24.30	$35.70	$35.70	$46.10
Tonnage entered (mil. NRT) [a]				
All flags	31.37	33.01	36.43	41.84
Italian flag	11.17	11.07	11.93	15.91
Foreign flags	20.20	21.94	24.50	25.93
Cargo unloaded (mil. MT) [b]				
All flags	21.66	27.20	27.76	31.28
Italian flag	9.38	10.54	10.18	14.81
Foreign flags	12.28	16.66	17.58	16.46
Cargo loaded (mil. MT)				
All flags	3.93	5.12	5.44	6.84
Italian flag	1.17	1.37	1.21	1.46
Foreign flags	2.76	3.75	4.23	5.38
Total cargo handled, foreign flags (mil. MT)	15.04	20.40	21.81	21.84
Japan				
Port receipts ($ mil.)	$13.10	$ 5.80	$17.10	$19.20
Tonnage entered (mil. NRT)				
All flags	23.10	14.45	17.83	22.35
Japanese flag	3.42	3.67	6.51	8.38
Foreign flags	19.68	10.78	11.33	13.97
Cargo unloaded (mil. MT)				
All flags		20.73	23.74	31.29
Japanese flag		6.37	11.46	14.33
Foreign flags		14.36	12.28	16.96
Cargo loaded (mil. MT)				
All flags		3.10	5.06	4.96
Japanese flag		.60	1.61	1.78
Foreign flags		2.49	3.45	3.18
Total cargo handled, foreign flags (mil. MT)		16.85	15.73	20.14
Port receipts per NRT				
Italy	$1.20	$1.60	$1.45	$1.75
Japan		0.55	1.50	1.35

SOURCE: Italy, *Statistica della Navigazione Marittima* (Instituto Centrale di Statistica), for 1950-1951, Table IV, for 1952-1953, Table VI; Japan, *Monthly Return of Foreign Trade*.
[a] Net register ton.
[b] Metric tons.

Amplification of the Records

From these figures it appears that the correspondence between port receipts and tonnages of foreign carriers is better than that between port receipts and cargo handled by foreign carriers. This is somewhat surprising, since income from handling the cargo usually exceeds the other group of port receipts. But there is, of course, some connection between tonnage and cargo unloaded or loaded, or both, although a rather loose one. However, the estimates for port receipts of Italy and Japan are based on tonnages rather than on total quantities of cargo handled.

Apart from the Japanese low 1951 figure, it appears that the average receipts were about $1.20 per NRT in 1950 and $1.50 for later years. On the assumption that the averages were lower in African countries because of lower labor costs, the averages for those countries were put at $0.75 per NRT for 1950 and $1.00 for later years. Multiplying these averages by the tonnages under foreign flags that visited the ports of certain countries yielded the figures shown in Table A-6. No port receipts were estimated for bunkering stations, since presumably oil companies do not charge separately for visits paid to their supplying facilities. Allocation of the receipts to paying areas was made in correspondence with the flag distributions of the tonnages loaded with cargo that visited the ports of each area, shown in Table A-7.

3

The Amplified Records

Apart from the additions described in the previous section, some adjustments were made. They fall mainly in one of two groups:

1. Some countries stated the c.i.f. value of their imports, and correctly increased their receipts from transportation by adding the freight on imports earned by their own ships. While this is the correct method for all c.i.f. reporting countries with ships bringing in part of their imports, only a few countries used it—Sweden, Colombia, Chile, Finland, and Yugoslavia. For the five countries, therefore, converting the value of imports from c.i.f. to f.o.b. required that the receipts from transportation be reduced by subtracting the freight on imports earned by their own carriers.

2. Other countries with sizable fleets reported only the net amounts of foreign exchange earned by their ships—India, Belgium, Greece, the Netherlands, and Argentina being the important ones. The net amounts had to be converted into gross freight earnings and disbursements abroad on the basis of information supplied by some of them (the Netherlands, for instance) or in the way described in the previous section for Greece.

There were also some minor increases and decreases for omissions or double counting. An example of the latter is the reporting by Egypt of freight paid to foreign carriers in its transportation debits, and at the same time its imports valued c.i.f.

To suggest the additions and subtractions made for each of the four years under study, a full account for 1951, the base year, is given in Table 20, starting with the figures shown in Table 3.

Comparing the new 1951 transportation figures with those of Tables 3 and 4, we see that the additions and subtractions resulted in widening the gap between receipts and payments from $312 million to $1,041 million, or by $729 million. Thus, we can conclude that the understate-

The Amplified Records

TABLE 20

ADJUSTMENTS IN TRANSPORTATION FIGURES, 1951
(millions of U.S. dollars)

RECEIPTS			
Original total [a]			5,437
Freight on imports earned by own carriers [b]		−118	
U.K. tanker fleet [c]	377		
Pan. Hon. Lib. fleet [d]	526		
Greek fleet, extra [e]	130	1,033	
Fuel from bunkers [f]	611		
Port dues, etc. [g]	144	755	
Other corrections		302	1,972
New total [h]			7,409
PAYMENTS			
Original total [i]			5,749
Freight on imports [j]		1,838	
U.K. tanker fleet [c]	317		
Pan. Hon. Lib. fleet [d]	304		
Greek fleet [k]	107	728	
Other corrections		135	2,701
New total [h]			8,450

[a] Table 3.
[b] Table A-1, 1951, indicated by *.
[c] Table A-3, 1951.
[d] Table A-4, 1951.
[e] Section 2, The Greek fleet.
[f] Table A-6, 1951.
[g] Table A-7, 1951.
[h] Table A-8, 1951.
[i] Table 4.
[j] Table A-1, 1951.
[k] Table A-5, 1951.

ment of receipts as well as payments, previously mentioned, obscured seriously the real deficiencies in the world transportation account.

The new totals for all transportation transactions in the four years of the study and their allocation are shown in Table A-8. The comparisons afforded by that table show, in all years, big surpluses of payments over receipts for all transportation items. The totals and differences are given below, in millions of dollars.

	1950	*1951*	*1952*	*1953*
Payments	5,656	8,450	8,713	7,555
Receipts	5,166	7,409	8,005	7,120
Difference	490	1,041	708	435

The differences must be considered in the light of the following:

1. Attempts to correct the balances of payments were limited to removal of some of the biggest gaps, and all the inaccuracies with which the

The Amplified Records

figures submitted by the countries are afflicted are reflected in the differences.

2. The receipts and payments of Soviet bloc countries, which are not members of the International Monetary Fund, are not included in the figures. However, both payments and receipts between IMF member countries and Soviet bloc countries for transportation are included. It can hardly be assumed that the receipts of the Soviet bloc countries for transportation exceeded their payments, even if the sale of coal out of bunkers by a country such as Poland is taken into account. Rather, it is far more likely that they paid more for transportation to the free world countries than they received, which would mean that the discrepancy is still larger than the figures indicate. A way to eliminate this gap would be to conform the receipts and payments of the Soviet bloc countries to the payments and receipts of their partners. This could be done, however, only if the partner countries clearly indicated the amounts paid to and received from the Soviet bloc countries. This type of information secured in the future from the IMF member countries would be a valuable means of amplifying the records.

3. The likelihood of inconsistencies in the reporting, discussed at the beginning of the first section, injects another source of differences between payments and receipts for transportation. Since the submitted figures were not corrected, the inconsistencies are still there.

As a first step in the process of reducing the surpluses of payments over receipts, a breakdown of receipts was made. Gross freights, the most volatile element in transportation accounts, particularly in those disturbed years, were separated from other items—charter hire, port receipts and expenditures, passage fares, and so on. This was feasible, since at the request of IMF most countries report their gross freight receipts and payments, often also showing an allocation of them. Exceptions were the cases where the freight on imports had to be calculated and allocated to receiving countries by flag of carrier. In some cases, however, the allocation of gross freights had to be figured out on the basis of regional information on payments or receipts for all transportation transactions, or with the aid of other information on transportation supplied by the country itself, or both. There was, however, one notable exception, besides the Pan. Hon. Lib. and Greek fleets—the United Kingdom, which does not report gross freights received from or paid to foreign countries. But as observed in Table A-8, there is a rather good correspondence between the figures stated by the U.K. for receipts from all transportation items and those stated by the partner countries for total payments to the U.K. There is an equally good correspondence between payments of the U.K. and the partners' total receipts from the U.K. The comparison is summarized in Table 21.

TABLE 21

COMPARISON OF TOTAL RECEIPTS AND TOTAL PAYMENTS OF UNITED KINGDOM WITH TOTAL PAYMENTS AND TOTAL RECEIPTS OF PARTNER AREAS
(millions of U.S. dollars)

U.K. RECEIPTS AND PARTNER PAYMENTS

PARTNER AREA	1950 Receipts of U.K.	1950 Payments of Partners	1951 Receipts of U.K.	1951 Payments of Partners	1952 Receipts of U.K.	1952 Payments of Partners	1953 Receipts of U.K.	1953 Payments of Partners
Rest of £ area	583	486	735	686	807	650	615	513
Non-£ EPU	321	386	459	547	499	600	407	550
U.S. and Canada	129 [a]	164	183 [a]	198	175 [a]	248	128 [a]	222
L.A.[a]	72	88	114	157	105	145	80	107
Other areas	80	100	165	151	162	157	145	170
All areas	1,185	1,224	1,656	1,739	1,748	1,800	1,375	1,562

U.K. PAYMENTS AND PARTNER RECEIPTS

PARTNER AREA	1950 Payments of U.K.	1950 Receipts of Partners	1951 Payments of U.K.	1951 Receipts of Partners	1952 Payments of U.K.	1952 Receipts of Partners	1953 Payments of U.K.	1953 Receipts of Partners
Rest of £ area	183	199	249	231	254	244	194	221
Non-£ EPU	351	334	543	505	664	567	504	540
U.S. and Canada	151 [a]	145	207 [a]	216	209 [a]	224	153 [a]	181
L.A.[a]	51	62	100	110	93	116	76	105
Other areas	52	93	94	108	106	110	71	110
All areas	788	833	1,193	1,170	1,326	1,261	998	1,157

[a] The United Kingdom reports receipts and payments from the dollar area, which includes also some countries of Latin America. The estimated receipts and payments from the latter were transferred to the next line. Hence, Latin America stands here for all countries of that area, including also the fleets of Panama, Honduras, and Liberia.

The Amplified Records

Though the correspondence is far from perfect, the differences between the figures of the United Kingdom and those of its partners range between 2 and 6 per cent. For 1953, the differences are around 15 per cent; one should, however, keep in mind that the figures reported just after the close of a year are very unstable and liable to be greatly changed later.

On the basis of this generally good comparison, it has been assumed that the gross freight receipts and payments of the United Kingdom are equal to payments and receipts reported by the partner countries. By virtue of this assumption it was possible to set up complete matrixes for receipts and payments for gross freights, shown in Table A-9. The figures for other items, by definition the difference between all transportation items and gross freights, are shown in Table A-10. The receipts and payments of all the reporting countries are summarized in Table 22.

TABLE 22

COMPARISON BETWEEN PAYMENTS AND RECEIPTS
OF ALL REPORTING COUNTRIES, 1950-1953
(millions of U.S. dollars)

		Payments	Receipts	Differences
1950	All transportation	5,656	5,166	490
	Gross freight	3,305	2,726	579
	Other items	2,351	2,440	−89
1951	All transportation	8,450	7,409	1,041
	Gross freight	5,475	4,416	1,059
	Other items	2,975	2,993	−18
1952	All transportation	8,713	8,005	708
	Gross freight	5,297	4,440	857
	Other items	3,416	3,565	−149
1953	All transportation	7,555	7,120	435
	Gross freight	4,528	3,796	732
	Other items	3,027	3,324	−297

SOURCE: For the appropriate years, the following Appendix tables: all transportation, A-8; gross freight, A-9; other items, A-10.

It appears from the table that other items did not contribute at all to the surplus of total payments over total receipts. On the contrary, for those items receipts are in all years higher than payments, and the excess of total payments over total receipts would even be greater without them. It is clear, therefore, that efforts to reduce the difference between

The Amplified Records

payments and receipts for transportation should be concentrated upon gross freights.

The actual situation, as far as gross freights are concerned, is even worse than appears from Table 22. While the amounts paid by Soviet bloc countries for all transportation items have probably been larger than the amounts received, the payments of those countries for gross freights have almost certainly been higher than their receipts. Moreover, an assumption accounts for the perfect correspondence between the gross freights paid and received by the United Kingdom on one side and by its partners on the other side. Almost all other countries show, however, an excess of payments over partners' receipts for gross freights and a deficit of receipts over partners' payments, as shown later. If this relationship applied also to the United Kingdom, the difference between total gross freight payments and receipts would be still greater.

The excess of gross freight payments over receipts is open to several explanations. First, the countries that estimated the freight on their imports might have overstated it. (This could also be true of the c.i.f.-f.o.b. adjustments in Table 6, though these are on the whole more carefully made.) It is hard to say whether there is an upward bias in the reported payments for gross freights. Second, some important seafaring countries might have understated the gross freight earnings of their carriers, whether they are transoceanic ships, coasters, barges, trains, trucks, or airplanes. In most cases the gross freight receipts of ships will greatly exceed those of other carriers (see Sections 5 and 6 for discussion of methods for improvement of gross freight payments and receipts). Third, it is possible also, that, in estimating the earnings of the Pan. Hon. Lib. and Greek fleets, the assumptions erred in favor of too much tonnage operated on time charter and too little on voyage charter. This would mean that not enough has been added to gross freights, for there is quite a difference in the average gross earnings and still more in the average net earnings of ships operated on time charter compared with earnings on voyage charter (see Section 2, Table 10). However, since the freight earnings of the Pan. Hon. Lib. fleet calculated here exceeded the freight payments of its partners in every year except 1950 (see Table 23 below), such a maladjustment between tonnages on time and on voyage charter is not very likely.

After the comparison of total payments and receipts for all transportation items, for gross freight, and for the other items, the next step is to look at their allocation. For this purpose the area grouping of partners was made uniform. The United Kingdom, for instance, lumps all dollar transactions together, whether they refer to the United States and Canada or to countries in Latin America. In the new grouping the gross freights

The Amplified Records

of dollar L.A. countries were estimated and transferred to the Latin American group. The regrouping resulted in eight areas instead of the previous six. The nonsterling EPU area was divided into metropolitan countries and their overseas territories, to correspond with the sterling area. A special area for the fleets (not the countries) of Panama, Honduras, and Liberia was introduced to enable a comparison between receipts and payments of those fleets. The allocation of receipts was indicated in the appropriate part of Section 2; that of payments was based on the flag distribution of the partner countries.

The comparison made is between the receipts of each area, as they are reported by that area, and the payments to that area as they are reported by its partners. Table 23 shows the comparison for the four years under study for all transportation items, for gross freights, and for all other items. Some interesting features emerge from the table.

1. *United Kingdom.* The difference between payments and receipts is rather small except in the last year, a discrepancy perhaps attributable to the instability all first reported figures seem to have.

2. *Rest of sterling area.* A big surplus of receipts over payments in the other items is here the outstanding feature.

3. *Nonsterling EPU metropoles.* These countries account on the average for about 75 per cent of the difference in all transportation items, and the same can be said of the difference in the gross freights! This can no longer be attributed to the reporting of net instead of gross freight earnings by some of the countries in that group because of the adjustments made. Hence, there appears to be a persistent understatement, at least by some countries, of gross freight receipts of the area. The difference in the other items is in the other direction and relatively small, except in 1953 for reasons given above.

4. *Nonsterling EPU overseas territories.* Here we notice an excess of receipts over payments, mainly on account of the other items (see 2).

5. *United States and Canada.* The almost constant excess of receipts over payments for other items is in contrast to the figures for gross freights, which show a rather good correspondence in 1950 and 1953, but big surpluses of payments over receipts for the years between. More detailed discussion of this subject will be found in the last section.

6. *Fleets of Panama, Honduras, and Liberia.* Virtually all the difference is centered in the gross freights which show a deficit of receipts over payments in 1950 and a surplus in 1952 and 1953. Whereas the figures for payments are in general more reliable than for receipts, in this group both payments and receipts were estimated, and equally subject to error.

7. *Latin America.* The excess of payments over receipts seems to fall

The Amplified Records

TABLE 23

COMPARISON OF PAYMENTS REPORTED BY PARTNER AREAS
WITH RECEIPTS REPORTED BY THE AREA, 1950-1953
(millions of U.S. dollars)

	1950 Partner Payments	1950 Area Receipts	1950 Difference	1951 Partner Payments	1951 Area Receipts	1951 Difference
Area						
ALL TRANSPORTATION ITEMS						
U.K.	1,224	1,185	39	1,739	1,656	83
Rest of £ area	323	411	−88	458	477	−19
Non-£ EPU metropoles	1,938	1,482	456	2,886	2,283	603
Non-£ EPU OT's	83	153	−70	129	146	−17
U.S. and Canada	1,101	1,164	−63	1,785	1,708	77
Pan. Hon. Lib.	333	289	44	521	526	−5
L.A.	252	145	107	344	191	153
Other areas	402	337	65	588	422	166
All areas	5,656	5,166	490	8,450	7,409	1,041
GROSS FREIGHT						
U.K.	865	865	−	1,311	1,311	−
Rest of £ area	45	57	−12	79	72	7
Non-£ EPU metropoles	1,263	868	395	2,062	1,368	694
Non-£ EPU OT's	5	−	5	6	−	6
U.S. and Canada	641	622	19	1,216	1,058	158
Pan. Hon. Lib.	273	219	54	437	425	12
L.A.	63	37	26	98	62	36
Other areas	150	58	92	266	120	146
All areas	3,305	2,726	579	5,475	4,416	1,059
OTHER ITEMS						
U.K.	359	320	39	428	345	83
Rest of £ area	278	354	−76	379	405	−26
Non-£ EPU metropoles	675	614	61	824	915	−91
Non-£ EPU OT's	78	153	−75	123	146	−23
U.S. and Canada	460	542	−82	569	650	−81
Pan. Hon. Lib.	60	70	−10	84	101	−17
L.A.	189	108	81	246	129	117
Other areas	252	279	−27	322	302	20
All areas	2,351	2,440	−89	2,975	2,993	−18

(continued)

The Amplified Records

TABLE 23 (concluded)

	1952			1953		
Area	Partner Payments	Area Receipts	Difference	Partner Payments	Area Receipts	Difference

ALL TRANSPORTATION ITEMS

U.K.	1,800	1,748	52	1,562	1,375	187
Rest of £ area	480	527	−47	382	489	−107
Non-£ EPU metropoles	3,137	2,604	533	2,845	2,494	351
Non-£ EPU OT's	91	155	−64	82	161	−79
U.S. and Canada	1,689	1,673	16	1,286	1,386	−100
Pan. Hon. Lib.	499	595	−96	467	530	−63
L.A.	334	202	132	279	213	66
Other areas	683	501	182	652	472	180
All areas	8,713	8,005	708	7,555	7,120	435

GROSS FREIGHT

U.K.	1,290	1,290	–	1,076	1,076	–
Rest of £ area	97	45	52	68	54	14
Non-£ EPU metropoles	2,093	1,536	557	2,025	1,420	605
Non-£ EPU OT's	7	–	7	10	5	5
U.S. and Canada	1,023	920	103	650	669	−19
Pan. Hon. Lib.	392	458	−66	353	385	−32
L.A.	91	54	37	69	69	–
Other areas	304	137	167	277	118	159
All areas	5,297	4,440	857	4,528	3,796	732

OTHER ITEMS

U.K.	510	458	52	486	299	187
Rest of £ area	383	482	−99	314	435	−121
Non-£ EPU metropoles	1,044	1,068	−24	820	1,074	−254
Non-£ EPU OT's	84	155	−71	72	156	−84
U.S. and Canada	666	753	−87	636	717	−81
Pan. Hon. Lib.	107	137	−30	114	145	−31
L.A.	243	148	95	210	144	66
Other areas	379	364	15	375	354	21
All areas	3,416	3,565	−149	3,027	3,324	−297

mainly in the category of other items; an improvement over the years can, however, be observed.

8. *Other areas.* Here gross freights count for most of the excess of payments over receipts. Other items show a rather good correspondence after addition to receipts of amounts for the sale of fuel from bunkers and for other port activities.

4

Tentative Analysis of the Records

So far, the discussion has dealt with statistical problems only, showing to what extent the information is deficient and describing attempts to fill the gaps in the records. The outcome is still far from satisfying. There are still big differences between payments and receipts, particularly in gross freights. Toward further improvement of these records, the last two sections indicate some methods for correcting the stated figures.

Despite all the imperfections, however, a first attempt is made here to explore the economic meaning of the figures as they are now, particularly the relationship between freight earnings and size of fleets. This relationship is examined for the years under study on the basis of the present information on gross freight payments and receipts, defective as it still is.

The information on freight earnings, moreover, is not yet complete. So far we have dealt with balance of payment figures only, i.e., with gross freights paid and received in foreign currency. But there are also freight earnings in domestic currency, paid by the importers of a country to the shipowners of the same country. It is clear that only the sum of these two types of freight earnings can be compared with the size of the fleets.

From the estimated freight on imports, the part of it paid to domestic carriers was separated out (see Table A-1). While most countries report the freight on imports earned by their domestic carriers, there are two notable exceptions, the United Kingdom and France, which do not report any freight on their imports. However, the freight on imports of these two countries in the four years of our study was computed (see Section 5), and the part of it earned by domestic carriers was estimated, as described in Section 2.

The total freight earnings are shown in Table 24, which contains two sets of figures, differing only in the gross freight paid and received in

Tentative Analysis of the Records

foreign currency. What was paid to and received by domestic carriers is, of course, the same in both sections, because it was reported by the same country; foreign currency accounts for about 39 per cent of freight payments and about 48 per cent of freight receipts.

A summary of percentage earnings of the United Kingdom, the nonsterling EPU metropoles, and the United States with Canada, is shown in the following tabulation.

	Partners' Records				Area's Own Records			
	1950	1951	1952	1953	1950	1951	1952	1953
U.K.	27%	26%	25%	25%	31%	30%	28%	28%
Non-£ metropoles	36	36	38	42	31	31	33	36
U.S. and Canada	22	22	20	17	24	23	22	20
	85	84	83	84	86	84	83	84

It appears that the three areas accounted for about 84 per cent of total earnings, whether recorded by partners as payments or by areas as receipts. The U.K. accounts for an average of about 28 per cent of earnings. The 3 to 4 per cent differences between partners' records and the area's own records in the four years are caused solely by differences in the earnings of all the other areas during those years. The amounts earned by the U.K. are the same in both records, having been estimated on the assumption that U.K. receipts are the same as partners' payments (Section 3). The nonsterling EPU metropoles account for an average of about 35 per cent of earnings. In contrast to the U.K. and the U.S., that area shows higher percentages in the partners' records than in its own, possibly owing to understatement of gross freight earnings in the area's records. The United States and Canada account for an average of about 21 per cent of earnings.

Comparing the percentages over time, we observe a decrease for the United Kingdom up to 1952 and an even sharper decrease for the United States and Canada. The percentage of the nonsterling metropoles shows, on the other hand, a sharp increase since 1951. These changes have little meaning unless related to the size of fleets operated in those years. Table 24 shows also the fleets in thousands of GRT as well as the percentage of the total each area had. The figures are taken from the Statistical Appendix of *Lloyd's Register,* Table 1 of Section 6 or 7 for the appropriate years. Of the tonnage figures for the merchant fleets of the world as of July 1 of each year, those for the vessels that earned the gross freights shown in Table 24 were pertinent. Accordingly some were omitted: the fleets of the Soviet bloc countries, since these countries do not report

TABLE 24

COMPARISON OF ANNUAL GROSS FREIGHT EARNINGS WITH SIZE OF FLEETS AS OF
JULY 1
(amounts in millions of U.S. dollars; tonnages in 1,000 GRT)

Area	Foreign Currency	Domestic Currency	All Currency	% of Total	Size of Fleet [a]	% of Total
			1950			
	PARTNER'S RECORD OF PAYMENTS					
U.K.	865	364	1,229	27	18,318	27
Rest of £ area	45	20	65	1	2,069	3
Non-£ metropoles	1,263	376	1,639	36	20,908	31
Non-£ OT's	5	1	6	neg.	neg.	neg.
U.S. and Canada	641	346	987	22	14,378	21
Pan. Hon. Lib.	273	–	273	6	4,138	6
L.A.	63	32	95	2	2,287	4
Other areas	150	122	272	6	5,251	8
All areas	3,305	1,261	4,566	100	67,349	100
	AREA'S RECORD OF RECEIPTS					
U.K.	865	364	1,229	31	18,318	27
Rest of £ area	57	20	77	2	2,069	3
Non-£ metropoles	868	376	1,244	31	20,908	31
Non-£ OT's	–	1	1	neg.	neg.	neg.
U.S. and Canada	622	346	968	24	14,378	21
Pan. Hon. Lib.	219	–	219	5	4,138	6
L.A.	37	32	69	2	2,287	4
Other areas	58	122	180	5	5,251	8
All areas	2,726	1,261	3,987	100	67,349	100

Area	Foreign Currency	Domestic Currency	All Currency	% of Total	Size of Fleet [a]	% of Total
			1951			
	PARTNER'S RECORD OF PAYMENTS					
U.K.	1,311	582	1,893	26	18,657	25
Rest of £ area	79	32	111	1	2,076	3
Non-£ metropoles	2,062	580	2,642	36	22,537	30
Non-£ OT's	6	1	7	neg.	neg.	neg.
U.S. and Canada	1,216	430	1,646	22	18,347	25
Pan. Hon. Lib.	437	–	437	6	4,721	6
L.A.	98	90	188	3	2,365	3
Other areas	266	211	477	6	5,627	8
All areas	5,475	1,926	7,401	100	74,330	100
	AREA'S RECORD OF RECEIPTS					
U.K.	1,311	582	1,893	30	18,657	25
Rest of £ area	72	32	104	2	2,076	3
Non-£ metropoles	1,368	580	1,948	31	22,537	30
Non-£ OT's	–	1	1	neg.	neg.	neg.
U.S. and Canada	1,058	430	1,488	23	18,347	25
Pan. Hon. Lib.	425	–	425	7	4,721	6
L.A.	62	90	152	2	2,365	3
Other areas	120	211	331	5	5,627	8
All areas	4,416	1,926	6,342	100	74,330	100

(continued)

TABLE 24 (concluded)

1952

Area	Foreign Currency	Domestic Currency	All Currency	% of Total	Size of Fleet [a]	% of Total
PARTNER'S RECORD OF PAYMENTS						
U.K.	1,290	508	1,798	25	18,733	24
Rest of £ area	97	35	132	2	2,119	3
Non-£ metropoles	2,093	594	2,687	38	24,076	31
Non-£ OT's	7	1	8	neg.	neg.	neg.
U.S. and Canada	1,023	455	1,478	20	18,148	24
Pan. Hon. Lib.	392	–	392	5	5,115	7
L.A.	91	109	200	3	2,539	3
Other areas	304	228	532	7	6,206	8
All areas	5,297	1,930	7,227	100	76,936	100
AREA'S RECORD OF RECEIPTS						
U.K.	1,290	508	1,798	28	18,733	24
Rest of £ area	45	35	80	1	2,119	3
Non-£ metropoles	1,536	594	2,130	33	24,076	31
Non-£ OT's	–	1	1	neg.	neg.	neg.
U.S. and Canada	920	455	1,375	22	18,148	24
Pan. Hon. Lib.	458	–	458	7	5,115	7
L.A.	54	109	163	3	2,539	3
Other areas	137	228	365	6	6,206	8
All areas	4,440	1,930	6,370	100	76,936	100

1953

Area	Foreign Currency	Domestic Currency	All Currency	% of Total	Size of Fleet [a]	% of Total
PARTNER'S RECORD OF PAYMENTS						
U.K.	1,076	449	1,525	25	18,692	24
Rest of £ area	68	26	94	2	2,227	3
Non-£ metropoles	2,025	536	2,561	42	25,646	33
Non-£ OT's	10	1	11	neg.	neg.	neg.
U.S. and Canada	650	420	1,070	17	15,331	20
Pan. Hon. Lib.	353	–	353	5	5,820	8
L.A.	69	77	146	2	2,797	3
Other areas	277	166	443	7	6,917	9
All areas	4,528	1,675	6,203	100	77,430	100
AREA'S RECORD OF RECEIPTS						
U.K.	1,076	449	1,525	28	18,692	24
Rest of £ area	54	26	80	1	2,227	3
Non-£ metropoles	1,420	536	1,956	36	25,646	33
Non-£ OT's	5	1	6	neg.	neg.	neg.
U.S. and Canada	669	420	1,089	20	15,331	20
Pan. Hon. Lib.	385	–	385	7	5,820	8
L.A.	69	77	146	3	2,797	3
Other areas	118	166	284	5	6,917	9
All areas	3,796	1,675	5,471	100	77,430	100

neg. = negligible.

[a] From Statistical Appendix, *Lloyd's Register of Shipping*, Table 1 of Section 6 or 7 for the appropriate years. See the accompanying text for omission of fleets.

Tentative Analysis of the Records

the gross freight earnings of their fleets;[23] the "moth ball" fleet of the United States and tonnages chartered out to the military authorities. The vessels operating in the Great Lakes are, however, included since both the U.S. and Canada report freight payments to and freight receipts from the other. No adjustments were made, however, for tonnages of other countries that were laid up in those years, since information was lacking for most countries. But, judging by the available information, only very small portions of the fleets were laid up, and the error cannot be sizable.

Several questions remained. One was whether allowance should be made for the fact that the ratio between cargo ships and passenger ships is not the same for fleets of all countries, some of which—the United Kingdom and some European countries—have a higher portion than others of vessels engaged in passenger traffic. Since most passenger ships carry also a fair amount of cargo, no attempt was made to eliminate the tonnages of passenger ships. A possible solution would be to compare the sum of gross freight and passenger fares with the size of the fleets, but detailed information on passenger fares was not available. Another matter is that the gross freights reported as paid and received refer not only to transoceanic ships, but for some countries also to inland waterways, overland and air transportation. Here again, insufficient information on the freight earnings of such other means of transportation prohibited their elimination from gross freights.

From the size of fleets and the percentage each area had in the free world's active fleet, shown in Table 24, the percentages of that fleet owned by each of the three areas, selected for comparison of freight earnings, are compared in the following tabulation. It appears that the fleets of the three areas accounted for about 79 per cent of the world

	1950	1951	1952	1953
U.K.	27%	25%	24%	24%
Non-£ metropoles	31	30	31	33
U.S. and Canada	21	25	24	20
	79	80	79	77

fleet in those years, which is about 5 per cent lower than their share in the world freight bill. Also, the United Kingdom's share and that of the nonsterling EPU metropoles in the world fleet is in general smaller than their shares in earnings, whether the figures are taken from the partner's record or the area's own record of earnings. Apparently, at least some

[23] A small part of their earnings, paid by the reporting countries, is contained in the gross freight payments to other areas.

Tentative Analysis of the Records

of the countries of both areas manage to earn more per GRT, i.e., to operate their fleets more economically, than the countries of other areas do. The opposite is true of the United States and Canada whose actual operating fleets constitute a higher share of the world fleet than their share of earnings constitutes of total gross earnings.

With the data on size of fleets operating during the four years under study, we can now compare the changes in the percentages of earnings and of size of fleets, as shown in Table 24, and make these observations.

1. The United Kingdom shows a gradual decrease in its proportional earnings, which is smaller than the decrease in the proportional size of its fleet.
2. The nonsterling EPU metropoles show a much bigger increase over the years in their proportional earnings than in the proportional size of their fleets.
3. The United States and Canada show a much bigger decrease in their proportional earnings than in the proportional size of their fleets.
4. The Pan. Hon. Lib. fleet's increase in the proportional size of its fleet is not matched by an increase of its proportional earnings.

What do the differences in these proportional changes mean? Not much, so long as we are not in a position to split the gross freight earnings into two components—the freight earnings of tankers and those of dry cargo ships. For, there is quite a difference in the earnings of the two types of ships, particularly if they are operated on voyage charter, as shown in Section 2. And there were in those years rather big differences in the share of tankers in the total fleets of those areas, as shown in Table 25.

TABLE 25

TANKER TONNAGES AND PERCENTAGE PROPORTION IN CORRESPONDING
FLEETS OF WORLD AREAS, 1950-1953
(tonnages in 1,000 GRT)

Fleets of:	1950		1951		1952		1953	
United Kingdom	3,803	21%	4,084	22%	4,533	24%	4,656	25%
Rest of £ area	38	2	27	1	69	3	82	4
Non-£ metropoles	4,849	23	5,663	25	6,341	26	7,167	28
U.S. and Canada	4,740	16	4,642	16	4,678	16	4,746	16
Pan. Hon. Lib.	2,132	52	2,345	50	2,598	51	3,315	57
Latin America	517	23	575	24	684	27	750	27
Other areas	647	15	723	15	924	16	1,072	17
All free world	16,726	20	18,059	21	19,827	22	21,788	24

SOURCE: See Table 24, footnote a.

Tentative Analysis of the Records

It appears from the table that the proportion of tankers in the fleets of the United Kingdom and the nonsterling EPU metropoles developed in those years at about the same rate as in those of all free world countries. The percentage of tankers in the fleets of the United States and Canada, however, seems to have been constant in these years. In other words, while the other areas show an increase in the less remunerative part of their fleets, that share of the fleets of the United States and Canada remained constant. In connection with our observations on Table 24 about the changes in proportional earnings and size of the fleets in those years, further observations become still more probable: (1) The nonsterling EPU metropoles increased their earnings per GRT considerably more than the countries of other areas did; (2) The average earnings of the United States and Canada decreased in comparison with the earnings of the other area countries. These conclusions are, however, only tentative. Until we have the gross freight earnings split between tankers and dry cargo ships, and can compare the earnings and fleet sizes of the two classes of ships separately, more definitive conclusions are not possible.

As indicated in the part of Section 2 dealing with tankers operated by British oil companies, a careful computation was made of the freight on oil products imported by each country in 1951 and 1952. Two other kinds of data are needed for a more precise analysis of the records. The first is a computation of the freight just described for 1950 and 1953, which would give the best possible estimates of the world tanker freight bill in all four years. The second is the world freight bill on imported dry cargo, which is much more difficult to compute because of the great variety of products and their freight rates. The subject is discussed in the next section in connection with the results of the computations made for the United Kingdom and France in the four years of the study. Much more time will be needed, however, to compute the dry cargo freight bill in the same way for all other member countries, assuming that the necessary information on freight rates can be secured. Such a computation would certainly be more accurate than that based on estimates furnished by the countries. Then the assessed freight on imports must be allocated, by flags of vessels or any other available information on the nationality of carriers, to the countries that earned the freight. This would provide us with as good an estimate as possible of the freight earnings of each of the eight areas in each of the four years. Moreover, the earnings of all areas in any year would automatically be equal to the freight payments, thus eliminating the need for a distinction between partners' records and countries' own records.

There is still another obstacle to obtaining good comparisons between gross freight earnings and size of fleet—lack of better information on

Tentative Analysis of the Records

tonnages chartered to and from the member countries in those years. At present, both receipts and payments of some countries for charter hire are included, not in the receipts and payments for gross freights, but in those for other transportation items. The gross freights earned by the chartered vessels are, however, included in the gross freight receipts of the countries operating the chartered vessels. Hence, tonnages chartered should be transferred from owner countries to operator countries before comparing freight earnings and size of fleets.

So far, not much information is available on tonnages chartered to and from other countries, except the information supplied by Norway. None could be obtained on tonnages chartered to and from other countries by the United States or the United Kingdom, for example, and none on the part of the Pan. Hon. Lib. fleet let on charter in those years (hence, the assumptions necessary for computing the earnings of this fleet for gross freights and charter hire, Table 15). Consequently, the corrections of figures for chartering and tonnages, shown in Table 24, could not be made to reflect operator relationships rather than ownership. Strong assumptions about tonnages chartered to and from other countries—except Norway—were needed also to compare the average earnings of dry cargo fleets of countries that distinguish, at least, between earnings by dry cargo ships and by tankers (Table 31, page 82).

The prospects for securing better information on chartering are difficult to evaluate at present. It would be splendid if all seafaring countries could be persuaded to release the same type of information on chartering as divulged by Norway in all these years. But, failing that, if the IMF could succeed in collecting accurate information on the payments and receipts for charter hire as well as on their allocation, it would provide a basis for estimating the tonnages chartered to and from other countries. The tonnages could then be transferred from the owner to the operator countries, which would greatly improve the comparison between gross freight earnings and size of fleets. Until these corrections can be made, however, all conclusions regarding efficiency in the operation of ships can be only tentative.

5

Methods to Correct Freight Payments

One possible explanation for the excess of payments over receipts is that countries estimating the freight component in the c.i.f. value of their imports might have overstated the amounts. The amounts of freight and insurance deducted by those countries from their c.i.f. values were, in 1950, $1,293 million; in 1951, $2,296 million; in 1952, $2,078 million; and in 1953, $1,797 million.[24] It might very well be that the amount of freight included in these figures is overstated by $150 to 200 million, or about 1 per cent of the total c.i.f. value of imports of those countries.

In case of such overstatement of freight payments, how can they be corrected? The approach selected will depend upon the degree of accuracy desired in the figures and upon the amount of work that can be done.

The method applied in this study was described, with its virtues as well as its shortcomings, in Section 2 under freight on imports. The conclusion there was that the accuracy of the results obtained by use of rough freight factors is not high, particularly if the same freight factor is used throughout all years irrespective of the change in proportion of freight rate to c.i.f. value. The question remains, also, whether the freight factor used for a particular commodity is the proper one. To determine the average freight factor for a particular commodity transported between two specific countries in a certain period of time requires at least some notion of the actual freight rates during that period. Failing that, an estimate must be made on the basis of various criteria. Apart from the difficulty of determining appropriate freight factors for each commodity transported in a particular year, the proper selection of commodities for

[24] According to Table 5 of Herbert B. Woolley's paper, "Transactions between World Areas in 1951," presented for discussion at the Conference on International Economics, Princeton, April 1956.

Methods to Correct Freight Payments

the computation is an important factor. The sample should be representative from a transportation point of view if the result is to be applied to the whole group of commodities imported by that country.

Another and—from the standpoint of transportation—more promising approach consists of collecting information on the quantities of a particular commodity imported and multiplying them by the appropriate freight rates. This method is in keeping with that actually used to determine freight amounts and can be expected to render the most accurate estimates possible. That accuracy still depends, however, upon whether the samples on which the computations are based are sufficiently representative. Selection of the size of samples requires information on corresponding freight rates and the total quantity imported by each country in a particular year.

It is for this reason that the collection of information began with efforts to find the total quantity of dry cargo imported by each country in each of the four years of the study.[25] Sometimes that information was readily available, but often many conversions to the same unit—metric tons—were necessary. From the total quantity of imports of a country, commodities imported in large quantities were selected, for it may be assumed that those bulk commodities accounted for most of the freight paid by the importing country.

Admittedly the freight rate—the other determining factor—on bulk commodities is, on the average, lower than on commodities transported in smaller quantities, but the above statement about freight still holds. Moreover, the freight rates on bulk commodities are more subject to quick and severe changes and consequently account for most of the variations in the freight amounts—another reason for focusing attention upon them in selecting the samples. In general, the samples comprise 70 to 80 per cent of the total quantity imported by a country. That proportion was obtained usually by including all commodities imported in quantities of 5,000 metric tons or more. For smaller countries or those having very detailed trade classifications, imports in smaller quantities had to be included to obtain the desired coverage.

For 1951, the base year of the study, such selections were made for countries that require careful computations of the freight on their imports. In general it was found that the number of items was not unmanageable. A country like Brazil, for instance, with an import quantity of 5,500 metric tons of dry cargo from noncontiguous countries in 1951, required no more than 61 commodity items to cover about 76 per cent of the imported quantity. A very careful selection was made for Japan

[25] The study was confined to dry cargo because of Dwyer's companion study of petroleum products, previously cited.

Methods to Correct Freight Payments

because of its dominant position as importer in the Far East that year; the coverage was about 97 per cent requiring almost 200 commodity items.

For all years, selections covering 75 to 95 per cent of imported quantities were made for all countries that had c.i.f. trade records, whether or not they made the c.i.f. adjustments. They comprise about two-thirds of the total number of reporting countries.

To calculate the freight amounts, all that is needed besides the selection of imported commodities is the appropriate freight rates. Some of them, particularly tramp rates applying to transportation of commodities in bulk, are not difficult to obtain. In collecting them some notable institutions in the United States and Europe cooperated, making possible a store in our files of tramp rates for commodities, imported as well as exported in those four years by North America and northwest Europe from and to various areas of the world.

To the information already collected on dry cargo liner rates applying to the transportation of commodities in smaller quantities, liner rates on United States exports and imports to all other areas in the four years were added, thanks to the courtesy of the Maritime Commission in Washington. Rates on imports and exports of Spain, and rates on imports of northwest Europe from some countries in South America (Brazil), South Africa, the Persian Gulf, the Far East (Indonesia), and Australia are also at hand.

At present not all the needed information on freight rates is available: liner rates on exports from northwest Europe, for trade between countries in Asia, Africa, and South America, and certain tramp rates are still lacking. This means that the calculations are partly based on estimates of freight rates, rather than the actual rates. At this point, a distinction between tramp and liner rates will be useful.

Tramp rates are generally fixed on open markets where prices quickly reflect changes in demand and supply. Consequently, the freight rates that are established at those markets, apart from loading and unloading charges, are proportional to the extent that the offered services are used. The latter are mainly determined by the space occupied by a certain quantity of the commodity and by the distance of transport. From the relationship between those two factors, the desired freight rate on a shipment can be figured approximately by use of a rate for comparable space and distance.

Liner rates, on the other hand, are established on imperfect markets. Shipowners are usually organized in conferences that enforce the application of freight rates agreed upon by the members. The freight rates lie in the majority of cases between two boundaries. The upper boundary is determined by the amount that can be charged without making trans-

Methods to Correct Freight Payments

portation unprofitable for the owner of the commodity—"what the traffic will bear." It is usually determined by the difference in price at the place of loading and the place of unloading, assuming that such clearcut prices at both ends of the haul exist. The lower boundary is determined by the specific costs to the ship operator in transporting a particular commodity over a particular route. But the costs are not always sharply defined, particularly not in the case of joint supply. For example, cargo space may be offered from the United Kingdom to the Levant, and at the same time the space not needed for that cargo is offered from the U.K. to Italy. The effect of joint supply on the indefiniteness of specific costs, too well known to dwell upon, explains in large part the great variability in freight rates for the Mediterranean and Caribbean, for instance, especially those in the neighborhood of the minimum rates.

Lying between the two extremes, the actual freight rate is determined by competition—always present, actively or potentially. First, there are the tramps which at times enter the trade attracted by the high liner rates. Then there are always outsiders that try to benefit from the favorable situation created by the restrictive practices of the conferences. And last, but not least, there is also much envy and suspicion among the members of the conference itself. In view of all this, it is surprising that conferences are able to function; good economic reasons must explain their existence.[26]

It is obviously difficult, though not impossible, to estimate appropriate liner freight rates for some of the selected commodity items. Serious mistakes might be prevented by comparing the estimated liner rates of a particular kind with those for general cargo. Almost every conference has such a general cargo rate in its tariff books to apply to commodities for which no specific rate is quoted. Those rates give a good indication of the general level of rates set by a conference in a certain period.

General cargo rates are particularly suited for application to the unselected commodity items, those not included in the samples. An idea of those rates in the past can be obtained, for instance, from the Danish yearly publication *Danmarks Handels fløde og Skibsfart*,[27] in which Table 10a shows what has been earned per ton of cargo by Danish vessels over a large variety of routes. Freight earnings for particular commodities, for instance, citrus fruit from Spain to various West European countries, are sometimes given also.

---

[26] A good description of the economic factors that call for the creation of a conference and of the influence it exerts on freight rates in general and liner rates in particular can be found in Daniel Marx, Jr., *International Shipping Cartels*, Princeton University Press, 1953.

[27] *The Danish Merchant Marine and Shipping in 1951*, p. 103.

Methods to Correct Freight Payments

The general conclusion emerging from this discussion of freight rates is that calculation of the freight payments of a particular country is not prohibited by insufficient information on freight rates, so long as the matter is handled with care and knowledge of the trade. The reader is reminded that this discussion deals only with the possibilities of assessing the freight paid for transportation of dry cargo that is imported by a certain country. The amount of freight paid for imported petroleum products is much easier to assess, since there is only one publicly quoted freight rate charged in the past for transportation of all petroleum products along a certain route. As mentioned before, the freight on petroleum products imported by each country in 1951 has already been computed, and computations for the other years are planned. To examine and eventually correct the c.i.f.-f.o.b. adjustments of a particular country, therefore, requires computing also the amount of freight paid for the transportation of imported dry cargo.

Accurate computations have been made here for France and the United Kingdom, for all four years of the study. The reason for selecting these two countries is that they do not state the amounts paid to foreign carriers or earned by their own carriers for transporting their imported commodities. The best results were obtained for France, which gives a detailed flag distribution for its imports, whereas that information is poor for the United Kingdom. Therefore, a minute description of the method of obtaining the results for France is given first, followed by only a rough indication of the procedure for the United Kingdom.

The total quantity in metric tons of commodities imported by France in the four years of our study is stated in *French Import Statistics*.[28] From this total is first deducted the quantity of imported petroleum products, since the freight on it is separately calculated, as will be shown later; what is left is the quantity of dry cargo imported. Part of the latter came by land from continental European countries. To find the volume of land-borne imports from those countries, the volume that came by sea (shown in France's *Maritime Statistics*)[29] was subtracted from the total dry cargo imported. Most, though not all, of the land-borne imports originated in contiguous countries and, in the IMF system, does not call for a freight entry in France's balance of payments. Freight rates were therefore estimated for the rest of the overland cargo. In addition, a selection was made of the seaborne imports by country of export and commodity group, to serve as a basis for the detailed freight calculations. Table 26 illustrates the procedure.

[28] *Tableau Générale du Commerce Extérieur*, 1953, Tables 1 and 9.
[29] *Tableau Générale de la Navigation Maritime et des Transports*, for 1934 to 1953, Tables 1 to 4.

Methods to Correct Freight Payments

TABLE 26

COMPUTATION OF QUANTITY OF SEABORNE DRY CARGO
IMPORTED BY FRANCE, 1950-1953
(1,000 metric tons)

Imports	1950	1951	1952	1953
Total quantity	38,832	48,839	51,940	49,312
Petroleum products	14,533	18,686	21,358	22,475
Dry cargo	24,299	30,153	30,582	26,837
From Continent	11,875	12,565	13,345	14,041
By sea	1,650	1,162	1,496	1,847
By land	10,225	11,403	11,849	12,194
Seaborne dry cargo	14,074	18,750	18,733	14,643
Selection	11,995	16,911	17,332	13,270
Coverage	85%	90%	93%	91%
Number of items	222	300	311	314

The selection contains all commodity items shipped from a country in quantities of 5,000 metric tons or more in each of the four years, and covers about 90 per cent of all imported seaborne dry cargo. The number of items for all four years is 1,147, covering more than 60 million metric tons or, on average, somewhat more than 50,000 metric tons per item.

Once the selection was made, the question arose how much of each selected commodity was unloaded in Mediterranean ports and how much in Atlantic ports, since there is a great difference in the respective freight rates. This question could be answered by use of France's *Maritime Statistics* which gives a breakdown by quantity of the commodities unloaded at every port of some significance. As could be expected, most of the dry cargo coming from Asia and from east and north Africa but only a small portion of the quantity from other areas was unloaded in Mediterranean ports.

The next step was to find the average freight rate for each selected commodity transported over a certain route for each of the four years—not too difficult, since we are rather well informed on freight rates for imports of western Europe. The unavailable freight rates were estimated along the indicated lines, taking account of differences in length of haul, stowage factor, and so forth. The freight rates were multiplied by the corresponding quantities to obtain the total amount of freight paid on about 90 per cent of the imported dry cargo.

The rest of the dry cargo, specified by country of export, consists

Methods to Correct Freight Payments

mainly of commodities usually transported by liners. To those quantities general cargo rates appropriate to each route were applied. Rates not available were estimated on the basis of the average freight rates of the selected items.

Finally, freight amounts paid on imported petroleum products were computed. No distinction between seaborne and not seaborne was necessary, but a distinction was made between the part that was directly loaded in the ports of the producing country and the part that went first by pipeline to another country before it was shipped. For this, France's *Maritime Statistics,* which indicates port of loading as well as port of unloading, was used. It was used also for the distinction between Mediterranean and Atlantic ports of unloading. It appeared that, unlike dry cargo, less than half of the imported quantity was unloaded in Mediterranean ports. Then the quantities were multiplied by the freight rate applicable to all sorts of petroleum products carried over a certain route, giving for each year the amounts of freight paid by France on petroleum products shipped from certain ports. A summary of the results is given in Table 27. Under (3), we observe the same fluctuations in the

TABLE 27

COMPUTED FREIGHT ON IMPORTS OF FRANCE, 1950-1953
(freight, millions of U.S. dollars; quantity, millions of metric tons)

	1950	1951	1952	1953
1. Selected Dry Cargo				
Freight	97.0	197.9	153.6	123.3
Quantity	12.0	16.9	17.3	13.3
Average freight	8.1	11.7	8.9	9.3
2. Nonselected Dry Cargo				
Freight	12.9	18.0	8.0	19.4
Quantity	2.7	3.6	1.5	2.2
Average freight	4.8	5.0	5.3	8.6
3. All Dry Cargo, Noncontiguous				
Freight	109.9	215.9	161.6	142.7
Quantity	14.7	20.5	18.8	15.5
Average freight	7.5	10.5	8.6	9.2
4. Petroleum and Derivatives				
Freight	95.2	191.2	253.2	150.3
Quantity	14.6	18.7	21.4	22.5
Average freight	6.5	10.2	11.9	6.7
5. All Imports, Noncontiguous				
Freight	205.1	407.1	414.8	293.0
Quantity	29.3	39.2	40.2	38.0
Average freight	7.0	10.4	10.3	7.7

Methods to Correct Freight Payments

freight amounts as shown by the rougher computations discussed in Section 2, under freight on imports. Though less sharp, the same fluctuations are noticeable in the average freight of all noncontiguous dry cargo. Comparing the last line under (3) and (4) we see that, whereas the average freight on dry cargo had its peak in 1951, for petroleum products its maximum was reached in 1952. This could be expected, since the tanker freight rates, applicable to most transported petroleum products, are based on the London Award, which is a two-year charter hire rate. Comparing the last lines under (1) and (2), we notice much more fluctuation in the average freight rate on the selected items than on the nonselected. This is also reasonable, since most of the selected items were carried by tramps, while the nonselected items were brought in by liners. That the average freight rate on the nonselected items is lower than that on the selected items is due to the fact that most of the nonselected items were shipped from nearby countries.

The amounts of freight on imported commodities computed by country of export had to be divided according to whether earned by French carriers or paid to foreign carriers. That division was based on the detailed information on the flags of the carriers, by country of loading and port of unloading in France (*French Maritime Statistics*). To be more precise, the quantities of cargo transported over each route by the carriers of the various flags was used as a basis for the division. The last step was to allocate the amounts earned by the foreign carriers to the eight areas adopted for the purpose of this study. The final outcome, specifying the amounts paid on its imports by France to its own and to foreign carriers, is shown below, in millions of U.S. dollars.

	1950	1951	1952	1953
Total freight on imports	205.1	407.1	414.8	293.0
Earned by own carriers	102.5	162.9	187.1	147.9
Paid to foreign carriers	102.6	244.2	227.7	145.1

It appears that, in the "normal" years 1950 and 1953, about half the amount of freight paid by France on its imports was earned by its own carriers; in the years between, however, their share was only about 40 per cent.

Essentially the same computations, described in detail for the imports of France, were made to find the total amount of freight paid by the United Kingdom on its imports. The final outcome is, however, far less accurate than that obtained for France, because the information on the flags of the vessels that carried the imported merchandise is so much poorer. The results are summarized in Table 28.

Methods to Correct Freight Payments

TABLE 28

COMPUTED FREIGHT ON IMPORTS OF UNITED KINGDOM, 1950-1953
(quantity in millions of metric tons; freight in millions of U.S. dollars)

	1950	1951	1952	1953
Quantity				
Total dry cargo imported	n.a.	n.a.	46.7	51.2
Selection	40.5	46.7	43.7	49.4
Coverage (%)	n.a.	n.a.	94.0	96.0
Number of items	697.0	797.0	709.0	799.0
Freight				
Calculated on selected dry cargo	374.0	667.0	497.0	528.0
Average [a]	9.3	14.3	11.4	10.7
Estimated on all dry cargo	396.0	708.0	530.0	548.0
On Petroleum and derivates	186.0	291.0	348.0	245.0
Total on imports	582.0	999.0	878.0	793.0
Earned by own carriers	364.0	582.0	508.0	449.0
Paid to foreign carriers	218.0	417.0	370.0	344.0

In this and following tables, n.a. = not available.
[a] U.S. dollars per metric ton.

The total quantity of dry cargo imported by the United Kingdom in 1950 and 1951 is, unlike that in 1952 and 1953, not stated in the OEEC publications on foreign trade. Overland traffic and contiguous countries were not problems in this case, but a breakdown of the imported quantities according to the port of loading would have been welcome. There is sometimes quite a difference in freight rates to ports on England's west coast, south coast, and east coast. Unlike the records for France, however, there is no flag distribution for each of these three areas—at least not published—and the assumption was made that most of the cargo coming from North America was unloaded at the west coast and the rest at the south or east coast with London as center.

The selection, as for France, contains all commodity items from a country in quantities of 5,000 metric tons or more; the coverage is about 95 per cent in the four years. The average number of items is about 750, with an average of about 60,000 metric tons per item, compared with the average for France of about 50,000.

The information on freight rates was sufficient to assign stated or estimated freight rates to all selected items. The average freight on the selected dry cargo for the United Kingdom is in general 20 per cent higher than that for France, because a large part of the quantity of

Methods to Correct Freight Payments

France's imports came from nearby overseas territories. The fluctuations in the average freight rate are similar to those for France, but more pronounced; moreover, the average freight rate in 1953 is lower than in 1952. The amount of freight paid on the nonselected items—about 5 per cent of all imported quantities—was estimated in an over-all way for all countries together. It was assumed to be equal to that on the selected items, probably somewhat on the high side. The freight on petroleum products was computed for 1951 and 1952, and for the other years was estimated along the lines indicated in Section 2, under tankers operated by British oil companies.

The total amount of freight on imports was next divided according to whether earned by British carriers and or paid to foreign carriers. Like the other allocations described here, this was based on the flags of the carriers, though information on flag distribution published by the United Kingdom is rather poor. The U.K., unlike France, releases no information on the flags of the carriers by country of loading or by groups of commodities, nor on the total quantity of commodities unloaded in British ports as a whole. A flag distribution of the tonnages of vessels that entered the British ports with cargo was available and was used as a basis for distributing the freight on imports over domestic and foreign carriers. It will be clear that the poverty of the information on the nationality of carriers has seriously affected the accuracy of the results.

6

Methods to Correct Freight Receipts

One method of correcting the freight receipts makes use of the checks that the system of reporting itself provides, i.e., what has been received by a particular country should be equal, theoretically, to the sum of the payments of its partners. Hence, if we had precise information on (1) the total amount of gross freight paid by each country on its imports in a certain year, and (2) the allocation of each country's freight payments to receiving countries, we could determine how much freight had been received by every seafaring country in that year.

In Section 5, the best that could be done to meet condition (1) was discussed at length. To meet condition (2) two ways are open: (1) to ask each country to report the gross freight it paid to each of its partners;[30] (2) to distribute, by one device or another, the freight payments among the receiving countries.[31] Method (2) was, however, rough in the sense that no distinction was made between groups of commodities nor between routes over which they were transported, often simply because the importing country does not publish a sufficiently detailed distribution by flag of carrier.

Quite a number of countries report very detailed data on the nationality of the carriers. France, as noted earlier, is the best example, but most countries of west and south Europe, and also some British Dominions (for instance, India and Australia) show many details about the flags of carriers. If more detailed information becomes available, it will be possible to improve to some extent the tentative allocation made so far. It would provide us with some kind of check on the freight receipts of sea-

[30] We may hope that the member countries will be able to meet this requirement not too far in the future.

[31] An example of such a distribution can be found in Section 2 under freight on imports, where the freight payments were allocated by flag of carrier of the cargo.

Methods to Correct Freight Receipts

faring countries that engage to only a small extent in chartering ships.

The method would, however, break down if applied to countries that charter or let on charter considerable amounts of tonnage each year for, in the majority of cases, if the carrier is let on charter, the flag is not changed to that of the operator. This causes a diversity in the allocation of the freight payments by flag of carrier. The method can provide, therefore, no more than a provisional check on the freight receipts of countries that are heavily engaged in chartering vessels. These countries are mainly the United Kingdom, the United States, the Scandinavian countries and, of course, the fleets of Panama, Honduras, and Liberia. To check their freight earnings we have to rely on the more subtle methods of comparing receipts over time and between fleets. Each method will be illustrated by an example.

COMPARISON OF FRENCH FREIGHT RECEIPTS OVER TIME

In Section 5, a description was given of the way in which the freight on imports of France was calculated and distributed between foreign and French carriers. In addition to the freight on imports paid to French carriers, there were also freight earnings on exports of France and on trade between third countries. Freight collected from countries outside the franc area may be assumed to be included in the receipts from maritime transportation as shown in France's balance of payments (with the possible exception of 1950, to be shown later). Freight earned by French carriers on commodities imported by the French overseas territories is, however, not included and had to be estimated as described before.

Payments for port services by French carriers to countries outside the franc area can be assumed to be part of the reported payments for maritime transportation. The rest went to foreign carriers as freight on imports of France, assumed to be equal to the results of the computations shown below. In addition to port disbursements in countries outside the franc area, there were port disbursements in the French overseas territories for refueling and other port activities, which were estimated by the method indicated in Section 2, under miscellaneous. These computations and estimates shown in Table 29, help us to form an idea of the financial gestures of the French fleet in those years.

In 1950, unlike later years, France's balance of payments does not specify receipts from transportation. The figure given as receipts from all transportation transactions is $25 million. That figure is substantially lower than the receipts from "transportation other than maritime" by $34 million in 1951, $38 million in 1952, and $40 million in 1953. Assuming that the $25 million reported in 1950 includes also receipts for "other

Methods to Correct Freight Receipts

TABLE 29

FRENCH FLEET FREIGHT EARNINGS AND PORT PAYMENTS
IN FOREIGN CURRENCY, 1950-1953
(millions of U.S. dollars)

	1950	1951	1952	1953
Freight earned on imports				
Of nonfranc countries	–	88	91	69
Of French OT's	49	84	97	79
Total	49	172	188	148
Of France	103	163	187	148
Port payments				
In nonfranc countries	63	66	65	48
In French OT's	23	41	47	41
Total	86	107	112	89
In France	n.a.	n.a.	n.a.	n.a.

transportation," nothing is left for freight earnings on imports of nonfranc countries in 1950. This seems very unlikely in comparison with the other years, and probably accounts for something like $50 million of the $395 million shown in Table 23 as the difference between gross freight payments and receipts in 1950.

COMPARISON OF SCANDINAVIAN AND UNITED STATES FREIGHT RECEIPTS

Another method of checking the amounts of freight received by the vessels of a particular country is by a comparison of average earnings. It is, however, a subtle method requiring a great deal of detailed information on the composition of the fleets as well as on their earnings. The composition affects earnings, for, as we have seen in Table 11, there is quite a difference between the average earnings of dry cargo ships and of tankers, and between average earnings within each group of ships on voyage charter and time charter. Hence, there must be sufficient information on earnings as well as on tonnages of all classes of ships in the fleet to determine its average earnings.

The average earnings of vessels operated by the residents of a particular country are of most interest from an economic point of view, since those earnings indicate to what extent the residents of that country were able to benefit from rises in freight rates and other changes in the constellation of freight markets. If, however, the owner lets his ship on charter, particularly for periods of several years, the average earnings

Methods to Correct Freight Receipts

are far less important from an economic point of view. A comparison of earnings of self-operated tankers would not be very interesting economically, because the petroleum trade is dominated by a small number of big oil companies in the United Kingdom and the United States, with sizable fleets of their own and much influence on tanker freights. The comparison chosen, therefore, is the average earnings of self-operated dry cargo vessels of some of the more important seafaring countries.

The best comparisons of this sort could be made for the three Scandinavian countries—Norway, Sweden, and Denmark. They all supply information separately on gross freight earned by self-operated dry cargo ships and by tankers. All except Denmark state also the tonnages of their fleets engaged in foreign trade and all except Sweden the tonnages chartered out to foreign countries. Table 30 illustrates the procedure of the comparison and the results obtained.

Norway shows in Table c of its publication *Norske Skip I Utenriksfart* the proportion of its fleet engaged in foreign trade at the end of the year, distributed by tankers, dry cargo ships, and passenger ships. For the comparison in Table 30, a simple average of the figures at the beginning and the end of the year was taken, rather than the annual averages shown in Norway's Table d which was used for estimating the freight earnings of the Pan. Hon. Lib. fleet (Table 11). In the computations for that fleet, due allowance was made for parts of a year when some ships were not in actual operation, a procedure yielding very accurate averages. However, since similar averages for the two other countries do not exist, the more simple computed averages were used for all three countries instead of the more accurate ones. Comparing the average tonnage in foreign trade according to Norway's Table c with the tonnage stated in *Lloyd's Register* as of July 1 of each year indicates that, in general, more than 10 per cent of the Norwegian fleet was not engaged in foreign trade, not even in 1951 and 1952 when the earnings in foreign trade were extremely high. The tonnages let on time charter to foreign countries were taken from Table d and increased proportionately. It was considered safe to assume that the tonnages chartered in those years by Norway from foreign countries could be neglected. Finally, the freight amounts earned on the imports of Norway, being part of the total earnings of the Norwegian fleet, are included in the gross freight earnings shown in Table 10. Earnings of the Swedish and Danish fleets also contain the freight amounts earned by them on the imports of their home countries.

Sweden specifies in Table N of its publication *Sjöfart* the various tonnages of its fleet engaged in foreign and coastal trade. For foreign trade, an average of the tonnages at the beginning and the end of each year was used, as for Norway. Comparing those averages with the ton-

TABLE 30

DERIVATION OF AVERAGE FOREIGN TRADE FREIGHT EARNINGS OF DRY CARGO VESSELS OPERATED BY RESIDENTS OF NORWAY, SWEDEN, AND DENMARK, 1950-1953 (tonnages in 1,000 GRT; earnings in millions of U.S. dollars)

	1950			
	Norway	Sweden	Denmark	Scandinavia
Tonnages				
Fleet, July 1 of year	5,457	2,050	1,269	8,776
In foreign trade [a]	4,715	2,015	1,291	8,021
Passenger ships [a]	84	210	101	395
Cargo vessels [a]	4,631	1,805	1,190	7,626
Tankers [a]	2,240	320	190	2,750
Dry cargo ships [a]	2,391	1,485	1,000	4,876
Laid up	–	–	50 [b]	50
	2,391	1,485	950	4,826
On time charter to other countries	781	n.a.	110	891
	1,610	1,485	840	3,935
On time charter from other countries	n.a.	n.a.	n.a.	n.a.
Self-operated dry cargo fleet	1,610	1,485	840	3,935
Earnings				
Gross freight	226	172	100	498
Gross freight, tankers	44	7 [b]	11	62
Gross freight, dry cargo ships	182	165	89	436
Average earnings [c]	113	111	106	111

	1951			
	Norway	Sweden	Denmark	Scandinavia
Tonnages				
Fleet, July 1 of year	5,817	2,116	1,344	9,277
In foreign trade [a]	5,057	2,081	1,367	8,505
Passenger ships [a]	87	217	101	405
Cargo vessels [a]	4,970	1,864	1,266	8,100
Tankers [a]	2,574	400	246	3,220
Dry cargo ships [a]	2,396	1,464	1,020	4,880
Laid up	–	–	20 [b]	20
	2,396	1,464	1,000	4,860
On time charter to other countries	746	n.a.	115	861
	1,650	1,464	885	3,999
On time charter from other countries	n.a.	n.a.	n.a.	n.a.
Self-operated dry cargo fleet	1,650	1,464	885	3,999
Earnings				
Gross freight	382	249	156	787
Gross freight, tankers	110	9 [b]	21	140
Gross freight, dry cargo ships	272	240	135	647
Average earnings [c]	165	164	153	162

(continued)

TABLE 30 (concluded)

	1952			
	Norway	Sweden	Denmark	Scandinavia
Tonnages				
Fleet, July 1 of year	5,907	2,334	1,391	9,632
In foreign trade [a]	5,327	2,256	1,439	9,022
Passenger ships [a]	93	223	98	414
Cargo vessels [a]	5,234	2,033	1,341	8,608
Tankers [a]	2,910	510	332	3,752
Dry cargo ships [a]	2,324	1,523	1,009	4,856
Laid up	–	–	19 [b]	19
	2,324	1,523	990	4,837
On time charter to other countries	769	n.a.	110	879
	1,555	1,523	880	3,958
On time charter from other countries	n.a.	n.a.	n.a.	n.a.
Self-operated dry cargo fleet	1,555	1,523	880	3,958
Earnings				
Gross freight	378	261	152	791
Gross freight, tankers	121	12	25	158
Gross freight, dry cargo ships	257	249	127	633
Average earnings [c]	165	163	144	160

	1953			
	Norway	Sweden	Denmark	Scandinavia
Tonnages				
Fleet, July 1 of year	6,264	2,578	1,529	10,371
In foreign trade [a]	5,800 [b]	2,417	1,520	9,737
Passenger ships [a]	95 [b]	232	95	422
Cargo vessels [a]	5,705	2,185	1,425	9,315
Tankers [a]	3,315 [b]	635	363	4,313
Dry cargo ships [a]	2,390	1,550	1,062	5,002
Laid up	–	–	35	35
	2,390	1,550	1,027	4,967
On time charter to other countries	775 [b]	n.a.	127	902
	1,615	1,550	900	4,065
On time charter from other countries	n.a.	n.a.	n.a.	n.a.
Self-operated dry cargo fleet	1,615	1,550	900	4,065
Earnings				
Gross freight	314	227	135	676
Gross freight, tankers	94	18	26	138
Gross freight, dry cargo ships	220	209	109	538
Average earnings [c]	136	135	121	132

[a] Averages.
[b] Estimates.
[c] U.S. dollars per GRT.

Methods to Correct Freight Receipts

nages as of July 1 of each year in *Lloyd's Register,* we see that, on the average, only about 2 per cent of Sweden's fleet was not engaged in foreign trade—a striking contrast to Norway. Without information on the tonnage for transportation of dry cargo chartered to and from foreign countries, the assumption was adopted that the tonnages both ways were the same in those years—probably not too far off. The average freight earnings for self-operated dry cargo vessels of Sweden arrived at were in all years somewhat lower than Norway's.

Since Denmark does not show in its publication *Danmarks Handels flØde og Skibsfart* the tonnage of its fleet engaged in foreign trade, the total tonnages stated for the beginning and the end of each year were used. This is probably why the average freight earnings arrived at for Denmark are 5 to 10 per cent lower than those obtained for Norway and Sweden. Denmark's Central Bureau of Statistics supplied information on the tonnages of dry cargo ships and tankers chartered out to foreign countries in those years. On the basis of the average charter hire received by the owners, it was assumed that all were dry cargo ships. As for Norway, it was assumed that the tonnages chartered from foreign countries can be ignored. The average freight earnings obtained for the Danish fleet were 5 to 10 per cent below those of the two other Scandinavian countries. However, if the fact that only part of the Danish fleet was engaged in foreign trade in those years could have been taken into account, average earnings arrived at for Denmark would probably have been about the same as found for Norway and Sweden.

In Table 30, the average earnings shown for the three countries together (Scandinavia) are probably somewhat lower than the actual earnings because of the lack of information about Denmark, just explained. Compared with dry cargo freight rates, the over-all average earnings not only change more gradually from one year to another, which is natural, but also have a somewhat different pattern, as the following indexes show.

	1950	1951	1952	1953
Average freight rate index	100	208	133	88
Average earnings index	100	146	144	119

The freight rate index is derived from *Norwegian Shipping News,* which computes and publishes monthly indexes of dry cargo rates, on trip charter (shown here) and voyage charter, separately, and of tanker rates for single voyages. It appears that the changes in the average earnings are not only smoother but also lag behind those of the average freight rates. Examination of the factors causing the difference in changes of freight rates and earnings would make an interesting separate study.

The United States is the other country for which a specification of the

Methods to Correct Freight Receipts

gross freights on U.S. exports, U.S. imports, and trade between third countries separately earned by dry cargo ships and tankers could be obtained. The information on the tonnages was sufficient to make a computation of average earnings similar to those for the Scandinavian countries possible. The amounts of gross freight earned by dry cargo ships on U.S. exports, including specified amounts earned in the coal and grain trade, were obtained from the *Survey of Current Business*.[32] Since no breakdown of the freight on military exports by tankers and dry cargo ships could be obtained, it was assumed that all this freight was earned by tankers. The amounts earned by dry cargo ships in trade between third countries and on U.S. imports was obtained from the Transportation Section, Balance of Payments Division, Department of Commerce. The freight received from Canada was subtracted from the totals, to be explained below.

The number of tons in actual operation in foreign trade during those years was taken from Maritime Administration publications. The assumed tonnage of the passenger fleet, 200,000 GRT in those years, was subtracted from the tonnage given for ships carrying passengers as well as cargo. Because of the special character of the Great Lakes trade, tonnages operating there were also excluded to make the comparison with Scandinavian countries as fair as possible.

No information could be obtained, however, on tonnages of freighters chartered from and to foreign countries in those years, but the charter hire received and paid by the United States for chartering of dry cargo vessels was supplied by the Commerce Department. Those amounts were converted to tonnages by use of the average amounts of charter hire received by Norwegian dry cargo ships in those years. The charter hire reported as received from foreign countries in 1950 was a multiple of the receipts in later years, probably because a large, but not exactly determined, amount of the 1950 receipts referred to later years. Some adjustment was made to counteract the adverse effect of that irregularity upon the average earnings.

Table 31 shows the tonnages of dry cargo ships engaged in foreign trade operations and their gross freight earnings in the four years, the last line showing the average earnings per GRT. A comparison of these average earnings with those of Scandinavian countries (Table 30) in millions of U.S. dollars is given below.

	1950	1951	1952	1953
Scandinavian countries	111	162	160	132
United States	130	141	133	131

[32] Published monthly by the Department of Commerce, Washington, D.C.

Methods to Correct Freight Receipts

TABLE 31

DERIVATION OF AVERAGE FOREIGN TRADE FREIGHT EARNINGS OF DRY CARGO SHIPS
OPERATED BY UNITED STATES RESIDENTS, 1950-1953
(tonnages in 1,000 GRT; earnings in millions of U.S. dollars)

	1950	1951	1952	1953
Tonnages in Foreign Trade, July 1 of Year				
Combined passenger and cargo	283 [a]	355 [a]	298 [a]	283 [a]
Freighters	3,696	5,589	5,133	3,458
	3,979	5,944	5,431	3,741
Chartered from other countries	432	403	426	512
	4,411	6,347	5,857	4,253
Chartered to other countries	50 [a]	212 [a]	162 [a]	27 [a]
Total	4,361	6,135	5,695	4,226
Gross Freight Earnings				
On commercial exports	335	629	503	332
On cross trade	26	28	32	24
On imports	225	249	274	241
	586	906	809	597
Received from Canada	19	38	53	42
Total	567	868	756	555
Average earnings, per GRT	130	141	133	131

[a] Adjusted.

The U.S. earnings were higher than the Scandinavian in 1950 but considerably lower in 1951 and 1952. Apparently the U.S. fleet benefited only slightly in 1951 by the favorable freight rate situation of 1951 and 1952, while the three Scandinavian countries showed good returns in both years.

There is a good possibility, however, that U.S. freighters earned more freight in 1951 and 1952 on U.S. exports and in cross trade than Table 31 indicates. The gross freights in Table A-9 show the following differences, in millions of U.S. dollars.

	1950	1951	1952	1953
Paid by partners to U.S. or Canada	644	1,219	1,022	649
Received by U.S. and Canada from partners	622	1,058	920	669
Difference	22	161	102	−20

Methods to Correct Freight Receipts

The considerable excess of partners' payments over the area's receipts in 1951 and 1952 may presumably be allocated in large part to U.S. dry cargo ships and tankers, rather than Canadian. Though not conclusive proof that the freight earnings of dry cargo vessels are understated for those two years, the differences strongly suggest that they are. Even so, the average earnings of U.S. dry cargo ships in 1951 and 1952 will remain well below the corresponding Scandinavian earnings, while those in 1950 remain above. In other words, in those years the U.S. average earnings seem to have been much more constant than the Scandinavian.

This constancy in the U.S. average earnings is not surprising in view of the various factors that favor it. First, some prevent the earnings from dropping too far down.

1. The U.S. fleet benefits greatly from the fact that every year enormous quantities of commodities are imported and exported by the United States in U.S. ships. This mitigates the reduction of earnings of the domestic fleet in a downturn, during which preference for the domestic flag is much stronger than in good times. The foreign trade of the Scandinavian countries is small compared with that of the United States, and the earnings of their fleets drop much more, therefore, in bad times. The amount of freight earned by U.S. carriers, both dry cargo ships and tankers, on the country's own imports and exports amounted in the four years to 85 per cent, on the average, of all U.S. freight earnings. The corresponding percentages were 18 per cent for Norway, 48 per cent for Sweden, 21 per cent for Denmark, and 29 per cent for all three Scandinavian countries.

2. The Foreign Operations Administration and its predecessors showed strong preference for shipping foreign aid items in U.S. operated vessels. It can be assumed that about $500 million was paid for freight by those agencies to U.S. flag vessels between April 1948 and June 1954.[33] While not all of it was freight on dry cargo, we can still assume that about $50 million was paid in each of the four years to U.S. freighters, most of it because of that cargo preference.

On the other hand, there is also a factor preventing the United States average freight earnings from rising above a certain level. The operations of virtually the whole U.S. dry cargo fleet are confined to thirty-one routes. The resulting greatly decreased flexibility of their operations prevents U.S. operators from taking full advantage of favorable freight situations, such as occurred in 1951 and 1952, towards increasing the earnings of their ships.

[33] Taken from Wytze Gorter, *United States Merchant Marine Policies: Some International Economic Implications* (Essays in International Finance No. 23, Princeton University, 1955), in which the United States shipping policies are sharply criticized.

Appendix Tables

Appendix Tables

TABLE A-1

ALLOCATION OF FREIGHT ON IMPORTS ESTIMATED BY NBER, 1950-1953
(millions of U.S. dollars)

Area Making Payments	Total Freight on Imports (estimated)	Domestic Carriers	Foreign Carriers	U.K.	Rest of £ Area	Non-£ EPU	U.S. and Canada	Pan. Hon. Lib.	L.A.	Other Areas
				1950						
Ireland	43	8	35	32		3				
Iceland	2		2	1		1				
New Zealand	67		67	49	8	1	8			1
Burma	11		11	8		2				1
Ceylon	21		21	12	1	5	2	1		
India	94	5	89	55	1	22	8	3		
Iraq	11		11	7		4				
Jordan	5		5	2		2				
Total other £	254	13	241	166	10	40	18	4	3	3
British OT's	210		210	98		69	19	10	3	11
Total £ area	464	13	451	264	10	109	37	14		14
Austria	35		35	1		23	4	1		7
Sweden	110	41	69	6		51	3	5		8
Switzerland	79		79	6		54	10		1	3
Turkey	21	4	17	4		9	2			2
Total continental EPU	245	45	200	17		137	19	6	1	20
French OT's	103		103	13		75	7	4		4
Netherlands OT's	30		30	11		3	15	1		
Portuguese OT's	10		10	3		7				
Total non-£ EPU	388	45	343	44		222	41	11	1	24

In this and other Appendix tables, Pan. Hon. Lib.—the fleet—is classified as an area.

(continued)

Appendix Tables

TABLE A-1 (continued)

(millions of U.S. dollars)

Area Making Payments	Total Freight on Imports (estimated)	Domestic Carriers	Foreign Carriers	U.K.	Rest of £ Area	Non-£ EPU	U.S. and Canada	Pan. Hon. Lib.	L.A.	Other Areas
Colombia	18	9	9	1		3	3	2		
El Salvador, Haiti	6		6			3	1	2		
Mexico	18		18	1		9	4	3	1	
Argentina	73	12	61	20	1	22	4	10	1	3
Chile	15	3	12	2		4	4	1	1	
Uruguay	14		14	5		5	1	2		1
Total Latin America	144	24	120	29	1	46	17	20	3	4
Finland	28	17	11	2		8		1		1
Yugoslavia	16	6	10	1		6	2	2		
Spain	51	37	14	3		8	1	3		
Spanish OT's	24		24	5		8	1	6		7
Total other Europe	119	60	59	11	1	30	4			8
Egypt	44		44	10		22	7			4
Iran	12		12	7		5				
Israel	29	4	25	4		11	3	4		3
Lebanon, Syria	19		19	4		9	2	3		1
Saudi Arabia, Anglo-Egyptian Sudan	12		12	5		5	2			
Total Middle East	116	4	112	30	1	52	14	7		8

Appendix Tables

Indonesia	26		26	6		15	2	1	2
Taiwan	14	3	11	3		3	3	1	1
Thailand	19		19	4		8	2	2	3
South Korea	11		11	2		3	5		1
Total Far East	70	3	67	15		29	12	4	7
Total other areas	305	67	238	56	1	111	30	17	23
Total all areas	1,301	149	1,152	393	12	488	125	62	65

1951

Ireland	59		49	43		6	1		
Burma	15		15	9	1	4	3		
Ceylon	33		33	20	1	9			4
India	182	10	170	91	2	42	29	2	
Iraq	14		14	9		4	1		
Jordan	5		5	2		2			
Total other £	308	12	286	174	4	67	34	2	1
British OT's	324	22	324	153	1	109	24	17	5
Total £ area	632	22	610	327	5	176	58	19	18
Austria	65		65	3		42	6	3	14
Sweden	202		141	11		106	5	7	16
Switzerland	117	61*	117	9		80	15	1	5
Turkey	31		25	6		12	3	1	3
Total continental EPU	415	6	348	29		240	29	11	38
French OT's	179	67	179	21		133	9	8	8
Netherlands OT's	49		49	19		3	26	1	
Portuguese OT's	13		13	3		10			
Total non-£ EPU	656	67	589	72		386	64	20	46

* See Table 20.

(continued)

Appendix Tables

TABLE A-1 (continued)
(millions of U.S. dollars)

Area Making Payments	Total Freight on Imports (estimated)	Domestic Carriers	Foreign Carriers	U.K.	Rest of £ Area	Non-£ EPU	U.S. and Canada	Pan. Hon. Lib.	L.A.	Other Areas
Colombia	21	11*	10	1		2	4	3		
El Salvador, Haiti	7		7			4	2	1	1	
Mexico	29		29	2		15	6	5	6	6
Argentina	192	35	157	36		61	25	23	1	
Chile	28	6*	22	4		7	8	2	9	1
Uruguay	26		26	6		10	4	4		7
Total Latin America	303	52	251	49		99	49	38		
Finland	67	31*	36	2		30	1	1		2
Yugoslavia	34	9*	25	3	1	12	7	2		1
Spain	65	36	29	2		12	8	6	1	
Spanish OT's	38		38	14		8	2	5	1	8
Total other Europe	204	76	128	21	1	62	18	14	2	11
Egypt	69		69	15		34	12			7
Iran	13		13	9		4				
Israel	43	7	36	4		18	5	3		5
Lebanon, Syria Saudi Arabia,	26		26	4	1	14	3	2		3
Anglo-Egyptian Sudan	22		22	8		10	3			1
Total Middle East	173	7	166	40	2	80	23	5		16

Appendix Tables

Indonesia	46		46	10		27	3	3		3
Taiwan	20		11	3		3	4	1		4
Thailand	25		25	6		11	2	2		1
South Korea	12		12	2		3	5	1		8
Total Far East	103		94	21		44	14	7		
Total other areas	480	92	388	82	2	186	55	26	2	35
Total all areas	2,071	233	1,838	530	7	847	226	103	14	111

1952

Ireland	46	8	38	32		6				
Burma	13		13	7	1	4	1			1
Ceylon	33		33	19	1	10	2			6
India	151	13	138	75	2	38	16	1		
Iraq	17		17	10		5	1	1		
Jordan	6		6	3		2				1
Total other £	266	21	245	146	4	65	20	2		8
British OT's	339		339	154		117	26	14	3	25
Total sterling area	605	21	584	300	4	182	46	16	3	33
Austria	54		54	2		32	10	3		10
Sweden	196	57	139	10		109	3	5		14
Switzerland	96		96	6		73	7			5
Turkey	39	4	35	9		18	3			5
Total continental EPU	385	61	324	27		232	23	8		34
French OT's	200		200	20		149	13	6		12
Netherlands OT's	60		60	23		4	33			
Portuguese OT's	16		16	4		12				
Total non-£ EPU	661	61	600	74		397	69	14		46

(continued)

* See Table 20.

Appendix Tables

TABLE A-1 (continued)
(millions of U.S. dollars)

Area Making Payments	Total Freight on Imports (estimated)	Domestic Carriers	Foreign Carriers	U.K.	Rest of £ Area	Non-£ EPU	U.S. and Canada	Pan. Hon. Lib.	L.A.	Other Areas
Colombia	23	12	11			4	5	1		1
El Salvador, Haiti	8		8			4	2	2		
Mexico	25		25	2		13	5	4	1	
Argentina	212	53	159	32		64	28	27	2	6
Chile	29	6	23	3		9	8	2	1	
Uruguay	22		22	4		9	4	4		1
Total Latin America	319	71	248	41		103	52	40	4	8
Finland	70	32	38	3		33	1	1		1
Yugoslavia	32	9	23	2		13	6	3		1
Spain	59	30	29	3		20	3	4		
Spanish OT's	39		39	11		12	2	4		10
Total other Europe	200	71	129	19		78	12	8		12
Egypt	61		61	9	1	33	10			8
Iran	8		8	5		3				
Israel	45	9	36	9		14	3	9		1
Lebanon, Syria Saudi Arabia,	23		23	5		11	2	5		
Anglo-Egyptian Sudan	35		35	14		15	5			1
Total Middle East	172	9	163	42	1	76	20	14		10

Appendix Tables

Indonesia	52	52	11		29	4	2		6
Taiwan	27	17	4		5	6	2		4
Thailand	27	26	5		13	2	2		1
South Korea	16	16	4		4	5	2		
Total Far East	122	111	24		51	17	8		11
Total other areas	494	403	85	1	205	49	30		33
Total all areas	2,079	1,835	500	5	887	216	100	7	120

1953

Ireland	44	36	30		6				1
Burma	8	8	4		2				1
Ceylon	34	34	19	1	11				7
India	110	104	57	1	30	2	1		1
Iraq	19	19	11	1	7	8			1
Jordan	6	6	3		2				
Total other £	221	207	124	3	58	10	1		11
British OT's	287	287	127	1	110	23	8	1	17
Total £ area	508	494	251	4	168	33	9	1	28
Austria	33	33	1		21	3			8
Sweden	137	97	7		77	2	1		10
Switzerland	71	71	4		58	2			
Turkey	38	36	10		18	3	3		4
Total continental EPU	279	237	22		174	10	4		5
French OT's	156	156	17		120	8	4		27
Netherlands OT's	29	29	11		3	14	1		7
Portuguese OT's	13	13	3						
Total non-£ EPU	477	435	53		307	32	9		34

(continued)

Appendix Tables

TABLE A-1 (concluded)

(millions of U.S. dollars)

Area Making Payments	Total Freight on Imports (estimated)	Domestic Carriers	Foreign Carriers	U.K.	Rest of £ Area	Non-£ EPU	U.S. and Canada	Pan. Hon. Lib.	L.A.	Other Areas
Colombia	27	16	11			4	4	2		1
El Salvador, Haiti	8		8	1		2	2	3	1	
Mexico	25		25	2		13	5	4	2	
Argentina	95	25	70	18		27	5	13	1	5
Chile	27	7	20	3		7	7	2		1
Uruguay	14		14	4		5	1	3		7
Total Latin America	196	48	148	28		58	24	27	4	
Finland	33	26	7	1		6		1		
Yugoslavia	32	8	24	1		10	11	4		1
Spain	43	20	23	3		14	2	4		3
Spanish OT's	44		44	29		7	1	4		3
Total other Europe	152	54	98	34		37	14	9		4
Egypt	44		44	8	1	24	5			6
Iran	6		6	4		2				
Israel	33		24	4		11	3	5		1
Lebanon, Syria Saudi Arabia,	35	9	35	7		16	4	7		1
Anglo-Egyptian Sudan	26		26	9		12	4			1
Total Middle East	144	9	135	32	1	65	16	12		9
Indonesia	44		44	9		24	3	2		6
Taiwan	23	8	15	4		5	5	1		
Thailand	30	1	29	5		14	3	1		6
South Korea	26		26	7		5	9	3		2
Total Far East	123	9	114	25		48	20	7		14
Total other areas	419	72	347	91	1	150	50	28		27
Total all areas	1,600	176	1,424	423	5	683	139	73	5	96

Appendix Tables

TABLE A-2

FREIGHT ON IMPORTS, STATED BY COUNTRY BUT ALLOCATED BY NBER, 1950-1953
(millions of U.S. dollars)

						Area Receiving Payments				
Area Making Payments	Total Import Freight	Domestic Carriers	Foreign Carriers	U.K.	Rest of £ Area	Non-£ EPU	U.S. and Canada	Pan. Hon. Lib.	L.A.	Other Areas
				1950						
Union of South Africa	81		81	47		21	7	4		2
Belgium	198	48	150	28	1	100	6	8		6
Italy	145	54	91	21		32	17	11	1	10
Netherlands	129	54	75	19		34	7	12		3
Norway	42	24	18	4		12				2
Total non-£ EPU	514	180	334	72	1	178	30	31	1	21
Costa Rica	4		4			1	1	2		
Dominican Republic	4		4	1		2		1		
Nicaragua	4		4			1	1	2		
Panama	8		8	2		2	4			
Venezuela	71		71	4		18	19	10	17	3
Paraguay	4		4	1		1			2	
Peru	33	3	30	5		8	12	2	3	
Total L.A.	128	3	125	13		33	37	17	22	3
Total all areas	723	183	540	132	1	232	74	52	23	26

(continued)

Appendix Tables

TABLE A-2 (concluded)

(millions of U.S. dollars)

Area Making Payments	Total Import Freight	Domestic Carriers	Foreign Carriers	U.K.	Rest of £ Area	Non-£ EPU	U.S. and Canada	Pan. Hon. Lib.	L.A.	Other Areas
1951										
Union of South Africa	117		117	60		34	14	7		2
Belgium	319	48	271	50		162	32	12	3	11
Italy	261	96	165	29	1	58	49	21	1	7
Netherlands	208	82	126	24		53	23	20	1	5
Norway	67	45	22	3		15	3			1
Total non-£ EPU	855	271	584	106	1	288	107	53	5	24
Costa Rica	5		5	1		1	1	2		
Dominican Republic	7		7	1		3	2	1		
Nicaragua	5		5	1		1	1	2		
Panama	8		8	2		2	4			
Venezuela	87		87	6		19	27	19	12	4
Paraguay	5		5	1		1	1	2		
Peru	48	3	45	8		12	18	3	4	
Total L.A.	165	3	162	20		39	54	29	16	4
Total all areas	1,137	274	863	186	1	361	175	89	21	30
1952										
Union of South Africa	118		118	63		35	12	6		2
Belgium	292	71	221	41	1	132	26	10	3	8
Italy	212	59	153	29		48	34	19	1	22

96

Appendix Tables

				1953					
Netherlands	201	72	129	24		59	13	26	1	6
Norway	56	35	21	3		14	2			2
Total non-£ EPU	761	237	524	97		253	75	55	5	38
Costa Rica	6		6	1		2	1	2		
Dominican Republic	8		8	1		4	2	1		
Nicaragua	7		7	1		2	2	2		
Panama	10		10	2		2	5	1		
Venezuela	95		95	3		29	36	9	13	5
Paraguay	8		8	1		2		1	4	
Peru	37	3	34	6		9	14	2	3	
Total L.A.	171	3	168	15		50	60	18	20	5
Total all areas	1,050	240	810	175	1	338	147	79	25	45
Union of South Africa	115		115	68		30	9	6		2
Belgium	296	94	202	38	1	136	8	10	1	8
Italy	229	74	155	34		55	22	19	1	24
Netherlands	182	56	126	27		65	3	24	1	6
Norway	56	35	21	2		16		1		2
Total non-£ EPU	763	259	504	101	1	272	33	54	3	40
Costa Rica	7		7			2	2	2	1	
Dominican Republic	4		4			2	1	1		
Nicaragua	7		7			2	2	2	1	
Panama	10		10	2		2	5	1		
Venezuela	95		95	5		29	35	12	6	8
Paraguay	6		6	1		1		1	3	
Peru	38	1	37	6		10	15	3	3	
Total L.A.	167	1	166	14		48	60	22	14	8
Total all areas	1,045	260	785	183	1	350	102	82	17	50

Appendix Tables

TABLE A-3
Receipts and Payments in Foreign Exchange by United Kingdom for Tanker Operations, 1950-1953
(millions of U.S. dollars)

		Area Making and Receiving Payments				
U.K. Receipts and Payments	All Areas	Rest of £ Area	Non-£ EPU	U.S. and Canada	Pan. Hon. Lib.	Other Areas
		1950				
Freight earnings						
British oil companies	187	70	107	6	–	4
Subsidiaries of U.S. oil companies	40	40				
Total receipts	227	110	107	6	–	4
Payments abroad						
Charter hire						
British oil companies	131		92	15	11	13
Subsidiaries of U.S. oil companies	27		11		16	
Other expenses						
British oil companies	66	25	38	2		1
Subsidiaries of U.S. oil companies	8	8				
Total payments	232	33	141	17	27	14
		1951				
Freight earnings						
British oil companies	307	113	178	10		6
Subsidiaries of U.S. oil companies	70	70				
Total receipts	377	183	178	10		6
Payments abroad						
Charter hire						
British oil companies	205		148	12	20	25
Subsidiaries of U.S. oil companies	42		17		25	
Other expenses						
British oil companies	62	23	36	2		1
Subsidiaries of U.S. oil companies	8	8				
Total payments	317	31	201	14	45	26

(continued)

Appendix Tables

TABLE A-3 (concluded)

(millions of U.S. dollars)

U.K. Receipts and Payments	All Areas	Rest of £ Area	Non-£ EPU	U.S. and Canada	Pan. Hon. Lib.	Other Areas
		1952				
Freight earnings						
British oil companies	384	163	190	9		22
Subsidiaries of U.S. oil companies	98	98				
Total receipts	482	261	190	9		22
Payments abroad						
Charter hire						
British oil companies	248		181	15	25	27
Subsidiaries of U.S. oil companies	54		27		27	
Other expenses						
British oil companies	86	37	42	2		5
Subsidiaries of U.S. oil companies	15	15				
Total payments	403	52	250	17	52	32
		1953				
Freight earnings						
British oil companies	243	116	109	8		10
Subsidiaries of U.S. oil companies	68	68				
Total receipts	311	184	109	8		10
Payments abroad						
Charter hire						
British oil companies	187		136	9	19	23
Subsidiaries of U.S. oil companies	48		24		24	
Other expenses						
British oil companies	58	28	25	2		3
Subsidiaries of U.S. oil companies	9	9				
Total payments	302	37	185	11	43	26

TABLE A-4

EARNINGS AND RUNNING EXPENSES OF VESSELS FLYING THE FLAGS OF PANAMA, HONDURAS, AND LIBERIA, 1950-1953
(millions of U.S. dollars)

P.H.L. FLEET RECEIPTS AND PAYMENTS	All Areas	U.K.	Rest of £ Area	Non-£ Metropoles	EPU OT's	U.S. and Canada	L.A.	Other Areas
1950								
Earnings								
On voyage charter								
Tankers	85							
Dry cargo vessels	134							
	219	27	28	31	5	42	53	33
On time charter								
Tankers	36							
Dry cargo vessels	34							
	70	7	–	9	–	54	–	–
Total	289	34	28	40	5	96	53	33
Running expenses								
On voyage charter								
Tankers	51							
Dry cargo vessels	106							
	157	19	20	21	4	30	39	24
On time charter								
Tankers	22							
Dry cargo vessels	26							
	48	7	–	9	–	32	–	–
Total	205	26	20	30	4	62	39	24
1951								
Earnings								
On voyage charter								
Tankers	182							
Dry cargo vessels	243							
	425	62	48	55	9	90	102	59
On time charter								
Tankers	48							
Dry cargo vessels	53							
	101	20	–	21	–	60	–	–
Total	526	82	48	76	9	150	102	59
Running expenses								
On voyage charter								
Tankers	74							
Dry cargo vessels	167							
	241	36	29	32	5	46	59	34
On time charter								
Tankers	25							
Dry cargo vessels	38							
	63	13	–	13	–	37	–	–
Total	304	49	29	45	5	83	59	34

(continued)

TABLE A-4 (concluded)

(millions of U.S. dollars)

P.H.L. FLEET RECEIPTS AND PAYMENTS	All Areas	U.K.	Rest of £ Area	Non-£ Metro- poles	EPU OT's	U.S. and Canada	L.A.	Other Areas
				AREA MAKING AND RECEIVING PAYMENTS				
				1952				
Earnings								
On voyage charter								
Tankers	207							
Dry cargo vessels	251							
	458	67	51	71	8	85	105	71
On time charter								
Tankers	65							
Dry cargo vessels	72							
	137	17	–	17	–	103	–	–
Total	595	84	51	88	8	188	105	71
Running expenses								
On voyage charter								
Tankers	88							
Dry cargo vessels	182							
	270	39	30	40	4	55	61	41
On time charter								
Tankers	34							
Dry cargo vessels	47							
	81	11	–	11	–	59	–	–
Total	351	50	30	51	4	114	61	41
				1953				
Earnings								
On voyage charter								
Tankers	178							
Dry cargo vessels	207							
	385	54	17	53	5	101	90	65
On time charter								
Tankers	90							
Dry cargo vessels	55							
	145	15	–	16	–	114	–	–
Total	530	69	17	69	5	215	90	65
Running expenses								
On voyage charter								
Tankers	104							
Dry cargo vessels	167							
	271	37	12	38	3	72	63	46
On time charter								
Tankers	53							
Dry cargo vessels	44							
	97	11	–	11	–	75	–	–
Total	368	48	12	49	3	147	63	46

TABLE A-5

EARNINGS AND RUNNING EXPENSES OF GREEK FLEET, 1950-1953
(millions of U.S. dollars)

GREEK FLEET RECEIPTS AND PAYMENTS	All Areas	U.K.	Rest of £ Area	Non-£ EPU Metropoles	EPU OT's	U.S. and Canada	L.A.	Other Areas
1950								
Earnings								
On voyage charter								
Tankers	2							
Dry cargo vessels	85							
	87	13	9	27	4	17	7	10
On time charter								
Tankers	3							
Dry cargo vessels	22							
	25	5	–	12	–	–	–	8
Total	112	18	9	39	4	17	7	18
Running expenses								
On voyage charter								
Tankers	1							
Dry cargo vessels	67							
	68	10	8	20	3	13	6	8
On time charter								
Tankers	2							
Dry cargo vessels	16							
	18	3	–	8	–	–	–	7
Total	86	13	8	28	3	13	6	15
1951								
Earnings								
On voyage charter								
Tankers	4							
Dry cargo vessels	122							
	126	19	13	38	6	25	11	14
On time charter								
Tankers	4							
Dry cargo vessels	27							
	31	7	–	14	–	–	–	10
Total	157	26	13	52	6	25	11	24
Running expenses								
On voyage charter								
Tankers	2							
Dry cargo vessels	84							
	86	13	9	26	4	17	8	9
On time charter								
Tankers	2							
Dry cargo vessels	19							
	21	5	–	–	9	–	–	7
Total	107	18	9	26	13	17	8	16

(continued)

TABLE A-5 (concluded)

(millions of U.S. dollars)

GREEK FLEET RECEIPTS AND PAYMENTS	All Areas	U.K.	Rest of £ Area	Non-£ Metropoles	EPU OT's	U.S. and Canada	L.A.	Other Areas
			1952					
Earnings								
On voyage charter								
Tankers	5							
Dry cargo vessels	116							
	121	18	13	36	6	23	11	14
On time charter								
Tankers	4							
Dry cargo vessels	33							
	37	9	–	17	–	–	–	11
Total	158	27	13	53	6	23	11	25
Running expenses								
On voyage charter								
Tankers	2							
Dry cargo vessels	84							
	86	12	10	25	4	17	8	10
On time charter								
Tankers	2							
Dry cargo vessels	22							
	24	6	–	11	–	–	–	7
Total	110	18	10	36	4	17	8	17
			1953					
Earnings								
On voyage charter								
Tankers	4							
Dry cargo vessels	91							
	95	15	10	29	5	18	8	10
On time charter								
Tankers	5							
Dry cargo vessels	24							
	29	6	–	14	–	–	–	9
Total	124	21	10	43	5	18	8	19
Running expenses								
On voyage charter								
Tankers	2							
Dry cargo vessels	73							
	75	11	8	23	4	14	7	8
On time charter								
Tankers	3							
Dry cargo vessels	19							
	22	4	–	10	–	–	–	8
Total	97	15	8	33	4	14	7	16

TABLE A-6

ESTIMATED RECEIPTS FOR SALE OF FUEL FROM BUNKERS ASSUMED NOT REPORTED, 1950-1953
(millions of U.S. dollars)

1950

Sales from Bunkers of:	Total Sales (1)	Domestic Carriers (2)	Foreign Carriers (3)	U.K. (4)	Rest of £ Area (5)	Non-£ EPU (6)	U.S. and Canada (7)	Pan. Hon. Lib. (8)	L.A. (9)	Other Areas (10)
Petroleum										
United Kingdom	94	68	26			19	3	2		2
Ceylon	12	–	12	7	1	3	1			
Iraq	1	–	1	1						
New Zealand	6	2	4	2		2				
	113	70	43	10	1	24	4	2		2
British OT's	168	28	140	66		48	15	2	4	5
Total £ area	281	98	183	76	1	72	19	4	4	7
Denmark	4	2	2	1		1				
France	19	8	11	3		4	1	1		2
Italy	14	6	8	2		3	1	1		1
Netherlands	18	10	8	2		3	1	1		1
Norway	4	3	1			1				
Sweden	3	2	1			1				
Switzerland	2	2	–							
	64	33	31	8		13	3	3		4
French OT's	28	13	15	4		8	3			
Netherlands OT's	94	–	94	19		34	23	9	9	
Portuguese OT's	8	–	8	3		5				
Total non-£ EPU	194	46	148	34		60	29	12	9	4
Argentina	16	3	13	4		4	2	2		1
Brazil	14	5	9	2		3	2	2		
Chile	1	–	1			1				
Colombia	3	1	2	1		1				
Cuba	2	–	2	1		1				
Mexico	18	–	18	2		7	5	2	2	
Peru	–	–	–							
Uruguay	5	–	5	2		2		1		
Venezuela	6	–	6	1		2	3			
Others	a									
Total L.A.	65	9	56	13		20	13	7	2	1
Spain	–									
Spanish OT's	41	–	41	10		14	1	4		12
Egypt	22	3	19	4		10	3	1		1
Iran	26	–	26	6		10	8	2		
Israel	2	2	–							
Saudi Arabia	13	–	13	3		5	4	1		
Sudan	1	–	1	1						
Indonesia	10	–	10	2	1	5	2			
Japan	9	2	7	1		2	3	1		
Philippines	3	1	2			1	1			
Total other areas	127	8	119	27	1	47	22	9		13
Total all areas	667	161	506	150	2	199	83	32	15	25
Coal										
Other £	1		1	1						
British OT's	6		6	1		2	1	1		1
Total £ area	7		7	2		2	1	1		1
Continental OT's	1		1			1				
Spain	5	3	2	1		1				
Spanish OT's	3		3	1		1	1			
Egypt	1		1	1						
Total other areas	9	3	6	3		2	1			
Total all areas	17	3	14	5		5	2	1		1

a Less than one-half million dollars.

(continued)

TABLE A-6 (continued)
(millions of U.S. dollars)
1951

Sales from Bunkers of:	Total Sales (1)	Domestic Carriers (2)	Foreign Carriers (3)	U.K. (4)	Rest of £ Area (5)	Non-£ EPU (6)	U.S. and Canada (7)	Pan. Hon. Lib. (8)	L.A. (9)	Other Areas (10)
Petroleum										
United Kingdom	126	89	37			26	5	4		2
Ceylon	15	–	15	9	1	4	1			
Iraq	2	–	2	1		1				
New Zealand	3	1	2	1		1				
	146	90	56	11	1	32	6	4		2
British OT's	189	32	157	71		55	13	6	5	7
Total £ area	335	122	213	82	1	87	19	10	5	9
Denmark	5	2	3	1		2				
France	48	19	29	10		9	5	2	1	2
Italy	25	8	17	3		6	6	1		1
Netherlands	37	12	25	6		9	5	4		1
Norway	8	6	2	1		1				
Portugal	9	3	6	2		3	1			
Sweden	7	4	3	1		2				
Switzerland	3	3	–							
	142	57	85	24		32	17	7	1	4
French OT's	58	28	30	7		14	4	2		3
Netherlands OT's	70	–	70	14		26	17	6	7	
Portuguese OT's	9	–	9	1		7	1			
Total non-£ EPU	279	85	194	46		79	39	15	8	7
Argentina	5	2	3	1		1	1			
Brazil	22	5	17	2		7	4	2	2	
Chile	1	–	1				1			
Colombia	3	2	1			1				
Cuba	2	–	2	1		1				
Mexico	4	–	4	1		2	1			
Peru	2	–	2			1	1			
Uruguay	6	–	6	1		2	2	1		
Venezuela	28	2	26	2		9	12	2	1	
Others	a									
Total L.A.	73	11	62	8		24	22	5	3	
Spain	8	5	3	1		1	1			
Spanish OT's	51	–	51	19		11	3	7	1	10
Egypt	9	2	7	2		4	1			
Israel	2	2	–							
Lebanon	12	–	12	3		7	2			
Saudi Arabia	21	–	21	2		4	11	3		1
Sudan	2	–	2	1		1				
Indonesia	13	–	13	3		7	1			2
Japan	22	6	16	3		5	6			2
Philippines	5	2	3	1			2			
Total other areas	145	17	128	35		40	27	10	1	15
Total all areas	832	235	597	171	1	230	107	40	17	31
Coal										
Other £	1		1	1						
British OT's	5		5	1		2	1			1
Total £ area	6		6	2		2	1			1
Continental OT's	2		2	1		1				
Spain	6	3	3	1		1	1			
Spanish OT's	2		2	1		1				
Egypt	1		1	1						
Total other areas	9	3	6	3		2	1			
Total all areas	17	3	14	6		5	2			1

a Less than one-half million dollars.

(continued)

TABLE A-6 (continued)
(millions of U.S. dollars)
1952

Sales from Bunkers of:	Total Sales (1)	Domestic Carriers (2)	Foreign Carriers (3)	U.K. (4)	Rest of £ Area (5)	Non-£ EPU (6)	U.S. and Canada (7)	Pan. Hon. Lib. (8)	L.A. (9)	Other Areas (10)
Petroleum										
United Kingdom	149	104	45			32	5	5		3
Ceylon	14	–	14	8		5	1			
Iraq	1	–	1	1						
New Zealand	3	1	2	1		1				
	167	105	62	10		38	6	5		3
British OT's	266	44	222	96		85	17	7	9	8
Total £ area	433	149	284	106		123	23	12	9	11
Denmark	9	3	6	1		4				1
France	59	22	37	14		13	5	1	1	3
Italy	28	9	19	4		6	5	3		1
Netherlands	39	12	27	6		10	6	4		1
Norway	8	6	2	1		1				
Portugal	9	3	6	2		3	1			
Sweden	8	3	5	2		3				
Switzerland	3	3	–							
	163	61	102	30		40	17	8	1	6
French OT's	61	32	29	6		17	2			4
Netherlands OT's	77		77	16		28	19	6	8	
Portuguese OT's	8		8	2		6				
Total non-£ EPU	309	93	216	54		91	38	14	9	10
Argentina	5	2	3	1		2				
Brazil	13	4	9	2		3	2	2		
Chile	2	1	1				1			
Colombia	1	1	–							
Cuba	2	–	2	1		1				
Mexico	5	–	5	1		3	1			
Peru	3	–	3			1	1	1		
Uruguay	6	–	6	1		3	1	1		
Venezuela	29	2	27	2		9	13	2	1	
Others	1	–	1			1				
Total L.A.	67	10	57	8		22	20	6	1	
Spain	8	5	3	1		1	1			
Spanish OT's	58	–	58	15		18	4	6		15
Egypt	26	3	23	5		12	4	1		1
Israel	1	1	–							
Lebanon	14	–	14	3		8	2	1		
Saudi Arabia	24	–	24	3		7	9	3		2
Sudan	2	–	2	1		1				
Indonesia	18	–	18	3	1	10	1	1		2
Japan	23	9	14	3		3	3	2		3
Philippines	6	2	4	1		2	1			
Total other areas	180	20	160	35	1	62	25	14		23
Total all areas	989	272	717	203	1	298	106	46	19	44
Coal										
Other £	1		1	1						
British OT's	3		3	1		2				
Total £ area	4		4	2		2				
Continental OT's	1		1			1				
Spain	6	3	3	1		1	1			
Spanish OT's	1		1			1				
Egypt	a									
Total other areas	7	3	4	1		2	1			
Total all areas	12	3	9	3		5	1			

a Less than one-half million dollars.

(continued)

TABLE A-6 (concluded)
(millions of U.S. dollars)
1953

Sales from Bunkers of:	Total Sales (1)	Domestic Carriers (2)	Foreign Carriers (3)	U.K. (4)	Rest of £ Area (5)	Non-£ EPU (6)	U.S. and Canada (7)	Pan. Hon. Lib. (8)	L.A. (9)	Other Areas (10)
Petroleum										
United Kingdom	139	97	42			29	4	5		4
Ceylon	11		11	6		4	1			
New Zealand	2	1	1	1						
	152	98	54	7		33	5	5		4
British OT's	210	35	175	66	3	67	15	10	7	7
Total £ area	362	133	229	73	3	100	20	15	7	11
Denmark	6	3	3	1		2				
France	46	18	28	9		10	4	1	1	3
Italy	28	16	12	3		4	3	1		1
Netherlands	35	13	22	5		8	5	3		1
Norway	7	4	3	1		2				
Portugal	9	3	6	2		3	1			
Sweden	6	2	4	1		3				
Switzerland	3	3	–							
	140	62	78	22		32	13	5	1	5
French OT's	49	26	23	6		12	1	1		3
Netherlands OT's	66	–	66	14		25	16	5	6	
Portuguese OT's	11	–	11	3		8				
Total non-£ EPU	266	88	178	45		77	30	11	7	8
Argentina	6	2	4	1		1	1	1		
Brazil	22	4	18	3		10	2	1	2	
Chile	2	1	1				1			
Colombia	1	1	–							
Cuba	2	–	2	1		1				
Mexico	4	–	4	1		1	2			
Peru	2	–	2			1	1	2		
Uruguay	5	–	5	2		2		1		
Venezuela	25	2	23	2		9	10	1	1	
Others	a									
Total L.A.	69	10	59	10		25	17	4	3	
Spain	8	5	3	1		1	1			
Spanish OT's	47	–	47	8	3	17	1	6		12
Egypt	21	3	18	4		10	2	1		1
Israel	4	4	–							
Lebanon	11	–	11	2		7	1	1		
Saudi Arabia	34	–	34	5		15	8	3		3
Sudan	2		2	1		1				
Indonesia	24	–	24	7		13	1			3
Japan	17	7	10	3		3	1	2		1
Philippines	7	2	5	1		2	2			
Total other areas	175	21	154	32	3	69	17	13		20
Total all areas	872	252	620	160	6	271	84	43	17	39
Coal										
Other £	a									
British OT's	2		2	1		1				
Total £ area	2		2	1		1				
Continental OT's	1		1			1				
Spain	5	3	2			1	1			
Spanish OT's	1		1			1				
Egypt	a									
Total other areas	6	3	3			2	1			
Total all areas	9	3	6	1		4	1			

[a] Less than one-half million dollars.

Appendix Tables

TABLE A-7

ESTIMATED PORT RECEIPTS, ASSUMED NOT REPORTED, 1950-1953
(millions of U.S. dollars)

Area Receiving Payments	All Areas	Rest of £ U.K. Area	Non-£ EPU	U.S. and Canada	Pan. Hon. Lib.	L.A.	Other Areas
			1950				
British OT's	34	16	11	3	2		2
French OT's	46	6	37	2			1
Portuguese OT's	10	3	7				
Belgian Congo	2		2				
Total non-£ EPU	58	9	46	2			1
Spain	6	1	3	1	1		
Spanish OT's	5	1	2	1	1		
Cuba	14	2	4	4	2	1	1
Philippines	6	1	2	2			1
South Korea	a						
Total other areas	31	5	11	8	4	1	2
Total all areas	123	30	68	13	6	1	5
			1951				
British OT's	36	16	12	2	2		4
French OT's	64	5	56	1			2
Portuguese OT's	10	3	7				
Belgian Congo	2		2				
Total non-£ EPU	76	8	65	1			2
Spain	6	1	2	2		1	
Spanish OT's	5	1	2	1	1		
Cuba	15	2	4	5	3	1	
Philippines	6	1	2	2			1
South Korea	a						
Total other areas	32	5	10	10	4	2	1
Total all areas	144	29	87	13	6	2	7

[a] Less than one-half million dollars.

(continued)

Appendix Tables

TABLE A-7 (concluded)
(millions of U.S. dollars)

Area Receiving Payments	All Areas	Rest of £ U.K. Area	Non-£ EPU	U.S. and Canada	Pan. Hon. Lib.	L.A.	Other Areas
			1952				
British OT's	39	17	16	2	1		3
French OT's	75	5	65	4			1
Portuguese OT's	10	3	7				
Belgian Congo	2		2				
Total non-£ EPU	87	8	74	4			1
Spain	9	2	4	2		1	
Spanish OT's	6	2	2	1	1		
Cuba	16	2	5	5	3	1	
Philippines	6	1	2	2			1
South Korea	a						
Total other areas	37	7	13	10	4	2	1
Total all areas	163	32	103	16	5	2	5
			1953				
British OT's	40	18	16	2	1		3
French OT's	73	7	60	4	1		1
Portuguese OT's	12	3	9				
Total non-£ EPU	85	10	69	4	1		1
Spain	11	2	4	3	1	1	
Spanish OT's	7	2	4	1			
Cuba	15	2	5	5	2	1	
Philippines	5	1	2	2			
South Korea	a						
Total other areas	38	7	15	11	3	2	
Total all areas	163	35	100	17	5	2	4

[a] Less than one-half million dollars.

Appendix Tables

TABLE A-8
Receipts and Payments, Revised, All Items and All Areas, 1950-1953
(millions of U.S. dollars)

Area Receiving Payments	U.K.	Rest of £ Area	Non-£ Metropoles	Non-£ OT's	U.S. and Canada	Pan. Hon. Lib.	L.A.	Other Areas	All Areas
1950									
RECEIPTS REPORTED BY AREA RECEIVING PAYMENTS									
U.K.	—	583	285	36	129	9	63	80	1,185
Rest of £ area	199	37	99	9	39	7	4	17	411
Non-£ metropoles	299	80	474	110	249	20	84	166	1,482
Non-£ OT's	35	—	71	—	28	9	9	1	153
U.S. and Canada	145	73	373	17	129	106	159	162	1,164
Pan. Hon. Lib.	34	28	40	5	96	—	53	33	289
L.A.	28	1	38	1	43	15	17	2	145
Other areas	93	5	132	1	65	11	5	25	337
All areas	833	807	1,512	179	778	177	394	486	5,166
PAYMENTS REPORTED BY AREA MAKING PAYMENTS									
U.K.	—	486	357	29	164	26	62	100	1,224
Rest of £ area	183	28	52	2	32	20	2	4	323
Non-£ metropoles	325	180	644	98	310	30	153	198	1,938
Non-£ OT's	26	3	40	2	7	4	1	—	83
U.S. and Canada	151	61	380	25	149	62	168	105	1,101
Pan. Hon. Lib.	42	31	48	5	102	—	68	37	333
L.A.	9	3	51	—	99	39	49	2	252
Other areas	52	23	174	4	72	24	9	44	402
All areas	788	815	1,746	165	935	205	512	490	5,656

Appendix Tables

1951

RECEIPTS REPORTED BY AREA RECEIVING PAYMENTS

U.K.	—	735	408	51	183	5	109	165	1,656
Rest of £ area	231	46	112	8	37	14	5	24	477
Non-£ metropoles	474	116	692	220	379	26	143	233	2,283
Non-£ OT's	31	—	72	—	23	8	7	5	146
U.S. and Canada	216	179	555	25	154	122	251	206	1,708
Pan. Hon. Lib.	82	48	76	9	150	—	102	59	526
L.A.	28	3	54	3	69	15	17	2	191
Other areas	108	19	146	1	72	12	17	47	422
All areas	1,170	1,146	2,115	317	1,067	202	651	741	7,409

PAYMENTS REPORTED BY AREA MAKING PAYMENTS

U.K.	—	686	501	46	198	49	108	151	1,739
Rest of £ area	249	52	70	3	40	29	1	14	458
Non-£ metropoles	509	287	960	173	352	45	239	321	2,886
Non-£ OT's	34	3	73	3	9	5	2	—	129
U.S. and Canada	207	107	662	42	181	83	327	176	1,785
Pan. Hon. Lib.	80	47	74	9	148	—	105	58	521
L.A.	20	2	90	—	109	59	57	7	344
Other areas	94	47	229	8	94	34	14	68	588
All areas	1,193	1,231	2,659	284	1,131	304	853	795	8,450

(continued)

Appendix Tables

TABLE A-8 (continued)
(millions of U.S. dollars)

1952

RECEIPTS REPORTED BY AREA RECEIVING PAYMENTS

Area Receiving Payments	U.K.	Rest of £ Area	Non-£ Metropoles	Non-£ OT's	U.S. and Canada	Pan. Hon. Lib.	L.A.	Other Areas	All Areas
U.K.	–	807	433	66	175	5	100	162	1,748
Rest of £ area	244	49	146	9	41	13	9	16	527
Non-£ metropoles	535	133	834	234	402	25	148	293	2,604
Non-£ OT's	32	–	79	–	25	6	8	5	155
U.S. and Canada	224	139	502	30	192	137	246	203	1,673
Pan. Hon. Lib.	84	51	88	8	188	–	105	71	595
L.A.	32	2	54	2	72	17	22	1	202
Other areas	110	21	192	8	96	19	9	46	501
All areas	1,261	1,202	2,328	357	1,191	222	647	797	8,005

PAYMENTS REPORTED BY AREA MAKING PAYMENTS

Area Receiving Payments	U.K.	Rest of £ Area	Non-£ Metropoles	Non-£ OT's	U.S. and Canada	Pan. Hon. Lib.	L.A.	Other Areas	All Areas
U.K.	–	650	546	54	248	50	95	157	1,800
Rest of £ area	254	56	69	–	43	30	1	27	480
Non-£ metropoles	625	316	1,013	198	383	51	262	289	3,137
Non-£ OT's	39	3	28	4	13	4	–	–	91
U.S. and Canada	209	91	527	57	200	114	321	170	1,689
Pan. Hon. Lib.	74	39	77	6	163	–	86	54	499
L.A.	19	3	67	–	122	61	62	–	334
Other areas	106	61	250	14	124	41	19	68	683
All areas	1,326	1,219	2,577	333	1,296	351	846	765	8,713

Appendix Tables

1953

RECEIPTS REPORTED BY AREA RECEIVING PAYMENTS

	U.K.	Rest of £ area	Non-£ metropoles	Non-£ OT's	U.S. and Canada	Pan. Hon. Lib.	L.A.	Other areas	All areas
U.K.	–	615	361	46	128	14	66	145	1,375
Rest of £ area	221	49	129	10	36	15	7	22	489
Non-£ metropoles	505	129	807	249	359	25	148	272	2,494
Non-£ OT's	35	–	84	–	25	7	6	4	161
U.S. and Canada	181	107	388	21	152	139	191	207	1,386
Pan. Hon. Lib.	69	17	69	5	215	–	90	65	530
L.A.	36	3	58	3	74	16	22	1	213
Other areas	110	21	183	3	81	15	10	49	472
All areas	1,157	941	2,079	337	1,070	231	540	765	7,120

PAYMENTS REPORTED BY AREA MAKING PAYMENTS

	U.K.	Rest of £ area	Non-£ metropoles	Non-£ OT's	U.S. and Canada	Pan. Hon. Lib.	L.A.	Other areas	All areas
U.K.	–	513	514	36	222	48	59	170	1,562
Rest of £ area	194	41	62	–	45	12	1	27	382
Non-£ metropoles	477	262	1,006	196	363	49	202	290	2,845
Non-£ OT's	27	3	31	7	9	3	2	–	82
U.S. and Canada	153	67	323	26	197	147	239	134	1,286
Pan. Hon. Lib.	63	15	63	5	176	–	86	59	467
L.A.	13	1	70	–	88	63	41	3	279
Other areas	71	49	252	9	141	46	20	64	652
All areas	998	951	2,321	279	1,241	368	650	747	7,555

Appendix Tables

TABLE A-9

RECEIPTS AND PAYMENTS, REVISED, GROSS FREIGHT, ALL AREAS, 1950–1953
(millions of U.S. dollars)

				Area Making Payments				
Area Receiving Payments	U.K.	Rest of £ Area	Non-£ Metropoles	Non-£ OT's	U.S. and Canada	Pan. Hon. Lib.	L.A.	Other Areas	All Areas

1950

RECEIPTS REPORTED BY AREA RECEIVING PAYMENTS

U.K.	–	455	177	29	69	–	56	79	865
Rest of £ area	4	32	5	7	–	–	–	9	57
Non-£ metropoles	121	58	245	102	131	–	75	136	868
Non-£ OT's	–	–	–	–	–	–	–	–	–
U.S. and Canada	42	55	169	16	72	–	152	116	622
Pan. Hon. Lib.	27	28	31	5	42	–	53	33	219
L.A.	4	1	6	1	13	–	11	1	37
Other areas	9	2	29	1	10	–	4	3	58
All areas	207	631	662	161	337	–	351	377	2,726

PAYMENTS REPORTED BY AREA MAKING PAYMENTS

U.K.	–	455	177	29	69	–	56	79	865
Rest of £ area	4	24	11	–	3	–	1	2	45
Non-£ metropoles	121	167	429	94	167	–	144	141	1,263
Non-£ OT's	–	3	–	2	–	–	–	–	5
U.S. and Canada	42	56	192	24	103	–	134	90	641
Pan. Hon. Lib.	27	31	48	5	57	–	68	37	273
L.A.	4	3	8	–	12	–	36	–	63
Other areas	9	21	57	4	14	–	7	38	150
All areas	207	760	922	158	425	–	446	387	3,305

Appendix Tables

1951

RECEIPTS REPORTED BY AREA RECEIVING PAYMENTS

U.K.	—	652	297	46	90	—	97	129	1,311
Rest of £ area	4	42	5	7	1	—	—	13	72
Non-£ metropoles	208	103	373	183	201	—	110	190	1,368
Non-£ OT's	—	—	—	—	—	—	—	—	—
U.S. and Canada	87	163	287	25	98	—	235	163	1,058
Pan. Hon. Lib.	62	48	55	9	90	—	102	59	425
L.A.	8	3	13	3	18	—	15	2	62
Other areas	15	17	48	1	11	—	13	15	120
All areas	384	1,028	1,078	274	509	—	572	571	4,416

PAYMENTS REPORTED BY AREA MAKING PAYMENTS

U.K.	—	652	297	46	90	—	97	129	1,311
Rest of £ area	4	40	26	2	3	—	—	4	79
Non-£ metropoles	208	274	745	164	189	—	217	265	2,062
Non-£ OT's	—	3	—	3	—	—	—	—	6
U.S. and Canada	87	99	436	38	115	—	276	165	1,216
Pan. Hon. Lib.	62	47	74	9	82	—	105	58	437
L.A.	8	2	29	—	20	—	37	2	98
Other areas	15	40	99	8	34	—	12	58	266
All areas	384	1,157	1,706	270	533	—	744	681	5,475

(continued)

Appendix Tables

TABLE A-9 (concluded)

(millions of U.S. dollars)

1952

Area Receiving Payments	U.K.	Rest of £ Area	Non-£ Metropoles	Non-£ OT's	U.S. and Canada	Pan. Hon. Lib.	L.A.	Other Areas	All Areas
RECEIPTS REPORTED BY AREA RECEIVING PAYMENTS
U.K.	–	611	298	52	109	–	88	132	1,290
Rest of £ area	4	25	3	6	1	–	–	6	45
Non-£ metropoles	239	102	430	199	214	–	124	228	1,536
Non-£ OT's	–	–	–	–	–	–	–	–	–
U.S. and Canada	68	117	220	26	120	–	231	138	920
Pan. Hon. Lib.	67	51	71	8	85	–	105	71	458
L.A.	6	2	10	2	14	–	19	1	54
Other areas	13	15	51	8	29	–	8	13	137
All areas	397	923	1,083	301	572	–	575	589	4,440
PAYMENTS REPORTED BY AREA MAKING PAYMENTS
U.K.	–	611	298	52	109	–	88	132	1,290
Rest of £ area	4	44	22	–	4	–	–	23	97
Non-£ metropoles	239	292	691	187	203	–	245	236	2,093
Non-£ OT's	–	3	–	4	–	–	–	–	7
U.S. and Canada	68	85	287	54	115	–	262	152	1,023
Pan. Hon. Lib.	67	39	77	6	63	–	86	54	392
L.A.	6	3	18	–	20	–	44	–	91
Other areas	13	50	94	13	56	–	18	60	304
All areas	397	1,127	1,487	316	570	–	743	657	5,297

Appendix Tables

1953

RECEIPTS REPORTED BY AREA RECEIVING PAYMENTS

	U.K.	Rest of £ area	Non-£ metropoles	Non-£ OT's	U.S. and Canada	Pan. Hon. Lib.	L.A.	Other areas	All areas
U.K.	—	493	267	35	86	—	52	143	1,076
Rest of £ area	3	32	4	8	—	—	—	7	54
Non-£ metropoles	213	96	396	200	193	—	113	209	1,420
Non-£ OT's	—	—	5	—	—	—	—	—	5
U.S. and Canada	51	83	115	20	96	—	169	135	669
Pan. Hon. Lib.	54	17	53	5	101	—	90	65	385
L.A.	8	3	11	3	30	—	13	1	69
Other areas	10	13	43	1	22	—	9	20	118
All areas	339	737	894	272	528	—	446	580	3,796

PAYMENTS REPORTED BY AREA MAKING PAYMENTS

	U.K.	Rest of £ area	Non-£ metropoles	Non-£ OT's	U.S. and Canada	Pan. Hon. Lib.	L.A.	Other areas	All areas
U.K.	—	493	267	35	86	—	52	143	1,076
Rest of £ area	3	32	12	—	4	—	—	17	68
Non-£ metropoles	213	254	780	173	193	—	185	227	2,025
Non-£ OT's	—	3	—	7	—	—	—	—	10
U.S. and Canada	51	60	114	24	121	—	174	106	650
Pan. Hon. Lib.	54	15	63	5	71	—	86	59	353
L.A.	8	1	16	—	15	—	29	—	69
Other areas	10	42	83	8	64	—	16	54	277
All areas	339	900	1,335	252	554	—	542	606	4,528

Appendix Tables

TABLE A-10
Receipts and Payments, Revised, Nonfreight Items, All Areas, 1950-1953
(millions of U.S. dollars)

Area Receiving Payments	U.K.	Rest of £ Area	Non-£ Metro-poles	Non-£ OT's	U.S. and Canada	Pan. Hon. Lib.	L.A.	Other Areas	All Areas
1950									
RECEIPTS REPORTED BY AREA RECEIVING PAYMENTS									
U.K.	—	128	108	7	60	9	7	1	320
Rest of £ area	195	5	94	2	39	7	4	8	354
Non-£ metropoles	178	22	229	8	118	20	9	30	614
Non-£ OT's	35	—	71	—	28	9	9	1	153
U.S. and Canada	103	18	204	1	57	106	7	46	542
Pan. Hon. Lib.	7	—	9	—	54	—	—	—	70
L.A.	24	—	32	—	30	15	6	1	108
Other areas	84	3	103	—	55	11	1	22	279
All areas	626	176	850	18	441	177	43	109	2,440
PAYMENTS REPORTED BY AREA MAKING PAYMENTS									
U.K.	—	31	180	—	95	26	6	21	359*
Rest of £ area	179	4	41	2	29	20	1	2	278
Non-£ metropoles	204	13	215	4	143	30	9	57	675
Non-£ OT's	26	—	40	—	7	4	1	—	78
U.S. and Canada	109	5	188	1	46	62	34	15	460
Pan. Hon. Lib.	15	—	—	—	45	—	—	—	60
L.A.	5	—	43	—	87	39	13	2	189
Other areas	43	2	117	—	58	24	2	6	252
All areas	581	55	824	7	510	205	66	103	2,351

Appendix Tables

1951

RECEIPTS REPORTED BY AREA RECEIVING PAYMENTS

U.K.	—	83	111	5	93	5	12	36	345
Rest of £ area	227	4	107	1	36	14	5	11	405
Non-£ metropoles	266	13	319	37	178	26	33	43	915
Non-£ OT's	31	—	72	—	23	8	7	5	146
U.S. and Canada	129	16	268	—	56	122	16	43	650
Pan. Hon. Lib.	20	—	21	—	60	—	—	—	101
L.A.	20	—	41	—	51	15	2	—	129
Other areas	93	2	98	—	61	12	4	32	302
All areas	786	118	1,037	43	558	202	79	170	2,993

PAYMENTS REPORTED BY AREA MAKING PAYMENTS

U.K.	—	34	204	—	108	49	11	22	428
Rest of £ area	245	12	44	1	37	29	1	10	379
Non-£ metropoles	301	13	215	9	163	45	22	56	824
Non-£ OT's	34	—	73	—	9	5	2	—	123
U.S. and Canada	120	8	226	4	66	83	51	11	569
Pan. Hon. Lib.	18	—	—	—	66	—	—	—	84
L.A.	12	—	61	—	89	59	20	5	246
Other areas	79	7	130	—	60	34	2	10	322
All areas	809	74	953	14	598	304	109	114	2,975

(continued)

Appendix Tables

TABLE A-10 (concluded)
(millions of U.S. dollars)

1952

Area Receiving Payments	U.K.	Rest of £ Area	Non-£ Metropoles	Non-£ OT's	U.S. and Canada	Pan. Hon. Lib.	L.A.	Other Areas	All Areas
RECEIPTS REPORTED BY AREA RECEIVING PAYMENTS								
U.K.	—	196	135	14	66	5	12	30	458
Rest of £ area	240	24	143	3	40	13	9	10	482
Non-£ metropoles	296	31	404	35	188	25	24	65	1,068
Non-£ OT's	32	—	79	—	25	6	8	5	155
U.S. and Canada	156	22	282	4	72	137	15	65	753
Pan. Hon. Lib.	17	—	17	—	103	—	—	—	137
L.A.	26	—	44	—	58	17	3	—	148
Other areas	97	6	141	—	67	19	1	33	364
All areas	864	279	1,245	56	619	222	72	208	3,565
PAYMENTS REPORTED BY AREA MAKING PAYMENTS								
U.K.	—	39	248	2	139	50	7	25	510
Rest of £ area	250	12	47	—	39	30	1	4	383
Non-£ metropoles	386	24	322	11	180	51	17	53	1,044
Non-£ OT's	39	—	28	—	13	4	—	—	84
U.S. and Canada	141	6	240	3	85	114	59	18	666
Pan. Hon. Lib.	7	—	—	—	100	—	—	—	107
L.A.	13	—	49	—	102	61	18	—	243
Other areas	93	11	156	1	68	41	1	8	379
All areas	929	92	1,090	17	726	351	103	108	3,416

Appendix Tables

1953

RECEIPTS REPORTED BY AREA RECEIVING PAYMENTS

	U.K.	Rest of £ area	Non-£ metropoles	Non-£ OT's	U.S. and Canada	Pan. Hon. Lib.	L.A.	Other areas	All areas
U.K.	—	122	94	11	42	14	14	2	299
Rest of £ area	218	17	125	2	36	15	7	15	435
Non-£ metropoles	292	33	411	49	166	25	35	63	1,074
Non-£ OT's	35	—	79	—	25	7	6	4	156
U.S. and Canada	130	24	273	1	56	139	22	72	717
Pan. Hon. Lib.	15	—	16	—	114	—	—	—	145
L.A.	28	—	47	—	44	16	9	—	144
Other areas	100	8	140	2	59	15	1	29	354
All areas	818	204	1,185	65	542	231	94	185	3,324

PAYMENTS REPORTED BY AREA MAKING PAYMENTS

	U.K.	Rest of £ area	Non-£ metropoles	Non-£ OT's	U.S. and Canada	Pan. Hon. Lib.	L.A.	Other areas	All areas
U.K.	—	20	247	1	136	48	7	27	486
Rest of £ area	191	9	50	—	41	12	1	10	314
Non-£ metropoles	264	8	226	23	170	49	17	63	820
Non-£ OT's	27	—	31	—	9	3	2	—	72
U.S. and Canada	102	7	209	2	76	147	65	28	636
Pan. Hon. Lib.	9	—	—	—	105	—	—	—	114
L.A.	5	—	54	—	73	63	12	3	210
Other areas	61	7	169	1	77	46	4	10	375
All areas	659	51	986	27	687	368	108	141	3,027

HOW TO OBTAIN
NATIONAL BUREAU PUBLICATIONS

National Bureau *books* are published and distributed by Princeton University Press; its *Occasional Papers* and *Technical Papers* are published and distributed by the National Bureau itself.

The National Bureau's publications may be obtained either on subscription or by purchase. Subscription rates are:

1. The standard subscription rate is $75 a year. A subscriber of this amount or more is entitled to receive one complimentary copy of each publication—*books, Occasional Papers, Technical Papers,* and the *Annual Report*—in advance of release to the public. In addition, the subscriber is entitled to a 33⅓ per cent discount on all National Bureau publications purchased.

2. A special subscription rate $35 is open to faculty members, students, and administrative officers of recognized educational institutions. A subscriber of this amount is entitled to receive one complimentary copy of each publication—*books, Occasional Papers, Technical Papers,* and the *Annual Report*—in advance of release to the public, and is entitled to a 33⅓ per cent discount on all National Bureau publications purchased. Only faculty members, students, and administrative officers of recognized educational institutions are eligible to become subscribers at the special rate.

3. A limited faculty-student rate of $5 is open to faculty members and students of recognized educational institutions. A subscriber of this amount receives a complimentary copy of each *Occasional Paper, Technical Paper* and the *Annual Report,* and is entitled to a 40 per cent discount on all publications purchased. Only faculty members and students of recognized educational institutions are eligible to become subscribers at the limited faculty-student rate.

4. The subscription rate for *Occasional Papers* and *Technical Papers* is $4 for five issues. A subscriber of $4 receives the next five *Papers* and the *Annual Report.*

NONSUBSCRIBERS: Order *books* from
Princeton University Press, Princeton, New Jersey

NONSUBSCRIBERS: Order *Papers* and request the *Annual Report* from:

SUBSCRIBERS: Order all *books* and *Papers* and request the *Annual Report* from:

NATIONAL BUREAU OF ECONOMIC RESEARCH, INC.
261 Madison Avenue   New York 16, N. Y.

Contributions to the National Bureau are deductible in calculating federal income taxes.